Talking with Patients

A Self Psychological View of Creative Intuition and Analytic Discipline

Sanford Shapiro, M.D.

JASON ARONSON INC.
Northvale, New Jersey
London

This book was set in 10 pt. New Century Schoolbook by Alpha Graphics of Pittsfield, New Hampshire, and printed and bound by Book-mart Press of North Bergen, New Jersey.

Library of Congress Cataloging-in-Publication Data

Shapiro, Sanford.
    Talking with patients : a self psychological view of creative
intuition and analytic discipline / by Sanford Shapiro.
      p. cm.
    Includes bibliographical references and index.
    ISBN 1-56821-598-3 (alk. paper)
    1. Psychoanalysis. 2. Intuition (Psychology) 3. Self psychology.
I. Title.
RC504.S47   1996
616.89'17—dc20   95-14483

Manufactured in the United States of America. Jason Aronson Inc. offers books and cassettes. For information and catalog write to Jason Aronson Inc., 230 Livingston Street, Northvale, New Jersey 07647.

To Anne, Beth, Lisa,
Jeff, Claire, and Neil

Contents

16—Hazards and Rewards   **185**

Acknowledgments

Much of my thinking has been influenced by two mentors: Bernard Brandchaft, M.D. and Robert Stolorow, Ph.D., and by two supervisors: James Fosshage, Ph.D. and Frank Lachmann, Ph.D. I want to thank all of my teachers and colleagues whose ideas I have assimilated.

I also want to thank my "editorial selfobject helpers": David Meltzer, Barbara Suzan Manalis, Lisa Shapiro, and Anne Reilly.

1

A Tale of
Two Theories

Art is exactitude winged by intuition.
Paul Klee

Psychoanalysis, like art, requires both precise technique and intuition. My teachers, being conservative, taught me technique, but did not trust me enough to encourage my intuition. They worried about *wild analysis*, a term introduced by Freud, who was concerned about technical errors and bad technique by unsophisticated and inexperienced analysts that could result in "dangers to patients . . . which are inherent in the practice . . . of a 'wild' psycho-analysis" (Freud 1910, p. 226). Concerns about wild analysis in psychoanalytic education have led to a reliance on rules, a stunting of spontaneity, and an inhibition of intuition.

The *Random House Unabridged Dictionary* defines intuition as "immediate apprehension": perceptions that are "independent of any reasoning process." Intuition, in other words, refers to a type of unconscious, creative activity. Intuitive analysts use their emotional experiences to enhance their understanding and inform their interpretations. My teachers used intuition in their practices, but it took me years to realize it. I thought they had formulas and rules that kept them on track. They always knew what to expect, what to say and what not to say. I believed that when I learned the rules, I would know the "right" way and avoid the "wrong" way. I didn't realize that what I did not do could have as much impact as what I did.

I now believe that the major challenge in psychoanalytic education and practice is to strike a balance between analytic discipline and creative intuition. Hoffman (1994) says that a dynamic relationship, a dialectic, always exists between spontaneous self-expression and analytic ritual. I believe that much of the tension between classical theory and self psychology is in how one maintains this balance.

CLASSICAL THEORY

The conservative nature of classical psychoanalytic education encourages "proper" analytic technique and discourages spontaneity. My first lesson in being proper was in 1959 during my first year of psychiatric residency at Detroit Receiving Hospital. There, immersed in diagnostic assessment, handling psychiatric emergencies, and managing medications, I began my first psychotherapy case, a young woman with depression and marital problems. I was pleased that my supervisor was psychoanalyst Frank Parcells, a wise, kindly man with an excellent reputation.

I had detailed process notes prepared for our first supervisory meeting that described how the patient came in to a session and said, "Hello, how are you?" "I'm fine," I answered, "and how are you?" Parcells interrupted me to ask, "Why did you say that?" "Well," I said, "It seemed the natural thing to do." Parcells gently explained that it would be natural in a social situation, but this was therapy, not a social situation. Thus I learned my first rule of proper technique. Each rule that I subsequently learned acted as a restraint, which led to an increasing rigidity in my style of working. My colleagues felt similarly restrained. This rigidity continued until the time of Kohut, when a shift occurred, and analysts began taking patients more seriously.

A reliance on cautiousness and rules was started by Freud's admonitions to analysts such as, "The doctor should be opaque to his patients and, like a mirror, should show them nothing but what is shown to him" (Freud 1912, p. 118), and analysts should "model themselves during psychoanalytic treatment on the surgeon who puts aside all his feelings, even his human sympathy . . ." (p. 115). Other "rules" suggested that the analyst must not "follow his expectations or inclinations" (1912, p. 112), or let the patient "leak" his material "with some intimate friend" (1913, p. 136).

Lichtenberg (1994) thinks that Freud used technical rules to deal with political problems; early adherents, among whom were Adler, Stekel, and Jung, did not follow Freud's theories. Although Freud trusted himself to be spontaneous, and could feed the Rat Man when he was hungry and organize financial support for the Wolf Man when he was destitute, he did not trust his students nor did he write down guidelines for being spontaneous or using intuition. So in the beginning, Freud determined what was proper analysis and what was not.

His death left us without an authority, and defining proper analysis now causes controversy, confusion, and anxiety. Many teachers play it safe and teach rules rather than what they do in their own practices. Sandler (1983) states that the fear of appearing "improper" has caused many analysts to keep much of their work secret from colleagues and students. Differentiating *public theory* from *private theory* Sandler says:

> The conviction of many analysts [is] that they do not do "proper" analysis . . . that what is actually done in the analytic consulting room is not "kosher", that colleagues would criticize it if they knew about it . . . that any analyst worth his salt will adapt to specific patients on the basis of his interaction with those patients. He will modify his approach so that he can get as good as possible a working analytic situation developing. I believe that the many

adjustments one makes in one's analytic work, including the so-called parameters that one introduces, often lead to or reflect a better fit of the analyst's developing intrinsic private preconscious theory with the material of the patient than the official public theories to which the analyst may consciously subscribe. [p. 38]

Sandler is saying that analysts are pleased with their work, but are reluctant to share what they do with colleagues and students because their intuitive creativity will be criticized.

SELF PSYCHOLOGY

Self psychology has brought new understanding to analytic interactions, has helped free analysts from the stricture of rules, and has helped them make sense out of what they had known intuitively and had done privately. I had thought that my job was to be the expert who understood, deciphered, and explained to patients their behaviors—to help them overcome their resistances and see things my way. I was taught to suspect a patient's motives, which left me feeling burdened. Self psychology, by teaching me the value of trusting patients' motivations and seeing things first from their perspectives, has freed me from much of that burden. One of my favorite quotes of Kohut (1984) follows:

If there is one lesson that I have learned during my life as an analyst, it is the lesson that what my patients tell me is likely to be true—that many times when I believed that I was right and my patients were wrong, it turned out, though often only after a prolonged search, that *my* rightness was superficial whereas *their* rightness was profound. [p. 93]

A common misperception of self psychology is that understanding someone's experience means you agree with it or condone it, but I have learned that understanding a patient's experience does not mean I have to give up my point of view. With self psychology I now have a theoretical framework in which I can teach creative intuition alongside analytic discipline.

Illustrating how self psychology has influenced my technique is a successful 35-year-old professional woman named Anna who entered psychoanalysis because of frustration with her inability to find a man with whom she could stay in love. Anna was in a relationship with Art, and they were living together. Although they cared deeply for each other, they could not stop fighting. Anna felt Art was trying to control her, and Art, when angry, said cruel things to her. Anna reacted either with violent rage—she wanted to hurt him—or with hopeless resignation—she wanted to leave him. She could not stand up for herself without being cruel.

In the analysis, the reasons for much of Anna's difficulty became clear: an older brother who abused and molested her, a mother who criticized and blamed her, and a father who kept his distance. She had learned early to wall off and disavow painful experiences. When feeling vulnerable with Art, she kept her distance, and when she felt overwhelmed, she lashed out at him in a violent rage. When she felt safe with me, she began to recall early experiences of rejection, hurt, humiliation, and shame.

She developed a new sense of confidence, and her professional life became even more successful, but, although she and Art became closer, their fighting continued. Each time Art hurt her, she felt betrayed and victimized, and her rage knew no bounds.

At that time, working in a classical mode, I felt it was my job to point out, and bring her face to face with, her contributions to the difficulty. I thought that the fighting would be resolved if she could confront Art without trying to destroy his self-esteem and if she could stay present and assert herself with him, instead of running away and hiding. My theory was that feelings from her past were being displaced onto Art, and that because of her resistance to the transference, Art had become the focus of her rage instead of me. Her resistance arose from internal pressures, and I was a blank screen that could observe but did not basically contribute to her resistance. My interpretations about her internal wishes and fears did not help, and as she became discouraged, I also became discouraged.

I had read some of Kohut's papers, but did not understand how to apply his ideas clinically. Then Bernard Brandchaft, a gifted teacher from Los Angeles, presented a series of lectures on self psychology in San Diego. He explained Kohut's ideas, and demonstrated their clinical applications. I immediately thought of Anna, and realized I had been trying to get her to understand what was going on from *my* point of view, and not trying to understand her experience from *her* point of view. Feeling pressured and criticized by my interpretations, she no longer felt safe. She was not resisting me; she was trying to protect herself in a way that I had not understood.

I also realized that I was not trusting her or the psychoanalytic process. I was trying too hard to "help" her and get her to see my point of view. I needed to decenter from *my* perspective, Brandchaft explained, and try to see things from the center of *her* experience, including my contributions to that experience.

I had been reluctant to do that, and thought that understanding how victimized, helpless, and vulnerable she was feeling would be condoning those attitudes and not encouraging her to take responsibility. I would not be doing my job of pointing out her contributions to the conflict, which stemmed from unconscious wishes. Brandchaft pointed out that understanding her point of view did not mean agreeing with it or approving of it, and if I could not understand her experience from her point of view, it was unlikely she would be able to understand my point of view.

I also had not appreciated the importance of maintaining a *listening perspective* (Schwaber 1981, 1983b). Ornstein and Ornstein (1985) state that "understanding . . . has either been taken for granted or seriously underplayed as a specific and necessary intervention in psychoanalysis . . ." (p. 44). Some patients require a long period of being heard and feeling understood before they are able to assimilate interpretations. Much strength and confidence often comes just from being listened to in an understanding way. Now I relaxed with Anna and listened patiently to her complaints, frustrations, and discouragements. I did not try to interpret or "fix" her pain, and limited my comments to appreciating how frustrated and discouraged she felt. As I stayed with her painful experiences, her discouragement progressed into despair and hopelessness. Although I did not feel hopeless, I appreciated how painful it was for her to feel hopeless. I told her, spontaneously, that I appreciated her being able to share such painful feelings with me.

She reacted to my comments with new memories of being molested and abused by her brother. She recalled that if she refused to do something he wanted, he held his hand over her mouth and nose, suffocating her, and when she was about to pass out, he let her breathe. Feeling terrified of him, she did what he asked. Adding to the trauma was her parents' unavailability; neither of them would tolerate any complaints. She had to keep her feelings to herself, and walled off all feelings of fear, hopelessness and despair. These feelings emerged anew in her relationships with Art and me. Being able to encounter and talk about these emotions with me was an integrating experience for Anna. She became stronger, her confidence returned, and her relationship with Art improved.

My attempts to explain her problem and "fix" her pain cut off her emerging affect, and inadvertently gave her the message that I, like her parents, did not want to hear her complaints. I had unwittingly become involved with her in reliving that traumatic experience. This shift to a new way of hearing clinical material is illustrated by Schwaber (1983a) when she describes "Kohut's most creative contribution":

> . . . the understanding of the resistance had shifted from being viewed as a phenomenon arising from internal pressures within the patient, from which the analyst, as a blank

screen, could stand apart and observe, to that in which the specificity of the analyst's contribution was seen as intrinsic to its very nature. [p. 381]

As I relaxed, I began to trust her, to trust the analytic process, and to trust myself. I worried less about rigidly following rules and reacted more spontaneously. I was pleased, not ashamed or apologetic, that I could spontaneously express my appreciation to her for being able to share her painful feelings with me. My appreciation was not contrived but something I genuinely felt. In self psychology lingo, I had provided her a validating, selfobject, developmental experience.

As a result of self psychology, a new openness has emerged in psychoanalytic practice. I first heard this acknowledged publicly in 1981 by Arnold Cooper, then president of the American Psychoanalytic Association. Cooper was the keynote speaker at the Fourth Annual Conference on the Psychology of the Self, and discussed the implications of self psychology for clinical practice. He told of the time he was called for a referral in another community, and not knowing any analysts there, he made some inquiries. He was given the name of a Dr. A with the comment, "He's a good analyst, but he is a little bit stiff." He wondered about that, made further inquiries, and was told about a Dr. B who was similarly described. Cooper remarked, "It seems that nowadays besides being competent, one also has to pass a certain stiffness test. This is something we weren't concerned about ten years ago."

I believe that analysts are able to loosen up, as I have done, without necessarily becoming "wild." I feel less pressure to know the answers, to be smart, and, not assuming I am a blank screen, I can then systematically look for my contributions to patients' transference experiences. Trusting them more, I ask more questions and make intuitive remarks more spontaneously. As a result, my patients do better, I enjoy my work more, and I can offer guidelines to students to help develop their intuition and creativity without derailing the psychoanalytic process.

Psychoanalytic education is a twofold process: it develops from within and from without. Freud developed the psychoanalytic method, *the talking cure*, from his work with patients. He learned from them and, as his clinical experiences grew, he developed and changed his theories. Like those of most students, many of his major discoveries resulted from therapeutic failures. For example, Freud discovered the importance of transference after his patient Dora, a 16-year-old girl, prematurely quit her analysis (Freud 1905).

Freud listened to colleagues and mentors, talked to patients, and, learning from his experiences, continued to develop and modify his theories. Richard Sterba, a graduate of the Vienna Psychoanalytic Institute, told me that his classmates felt a sense of betrayal when Freud (1926) announced the change in his theory of anxiety. "How can he do this do us?" they complained. "Just when we are starting to understand how things work, he turns everything upside down!"

Psychoanalytic students develop similarly, and following Freud's model, learn from both mentors and mistakes, change their ideas, and develop as they grow. No two psychoanalysts are the same, and each develops his or her own style. Students struggle to be like their mentors yet maintain their individual ways of working; and teachers struggle to show students what to do, yet encourage them to follow their own paths. "We eventually move beyond our models; we take what we need and then we shed those skins and become who we are supposed to become" (Zinsser 1988, p. 15).

In this book I will describe contributions from self psychology, selfobject theory, and intersubjectivity theory, and I will discuss technical guidelines for talking to patients—balancing rules with intuition.

2

The Role
of Theory

Courage: Grace under pressure.
Ernest Hemingway

Talking to patients exposes us to enormous pressures to understand what we are hearing, to be helpful, and to avoid being harmful. When we feel inundated by material we do not understand, we frequently become anxious, and our anxiety, if sensed by our patients, could be frightening to them. Staying calm, even when confused, is half the battle; staying emotionally connected with our patients is the other half.

Theory provides a structure that helps us organize our thinking, remain calm, and stay connected. Lindon (1991) says we need theories "to help us organize what otherwise is a chaotic jumble of meaningless material and to widen our perceptual scope" (p. 15). Staying connected with patients is hard when we doubt ourselves, but having a theory to anchor us, even one that challenges our own, helps us maintain that connection. It gives us the confidence to assure our patients that we will get through these difficulties together, even if we do not understand everything that is happening.

Although we have learned much about the psychoanalytic process, much that takes place in psychoanalysis is yet to be understood.[1] Therefore, we cannot take our theories for granted, but must be willing to question them, aware that while theory can help us, it can also hinder us. Theory, followed too closely, can lead to mechanical behavior and can stifle creativity. It can lull us into a false sense of security when we think we understand, and then encourage us to jump to conclusions and prematurely discontinue necessary psychoanalytic investigation. Knowing the next question may be more important than knowing the answer. The challenge "is to find a way, from deeply within ourselves, to come to terms with the idea that we do not know one more 'true' reality and that the patient's view, even about us, is as real as the one we believe about ourselves" (Schwaber 1983a, p. 390).

Theory, the way we understand clinical material, influences how we talk to patients, and is conveyed to patients by our attitudes and interpretations. Yet theory does not always translate into technique, and research shows that analysts from the same theoretical school may work very differently, while analysts from differing theoretical schools may work similarly (Hamilton 1991).

I was surprised to find much in common with experienced analysts from different theoretical schools in the way we talk to our patients. In dialogues where we presented cases to each other, many of our interpretations were similar. I believe that sensitive therapists use their intuition while looking for what works and what does not work. Over time, as they gain experience, these therapists rely less on theory and more on intuition and do more of what works and less of what does not work. A Radical-Behaviorist colleague told me he believes that therapists are conditioned by their patients. Self psychology has changed the way I understand clinical material. It has influenced my technique in (1) the shifting to a two-person psychology model and (2) the understanding and interpretation of motivation and resistance.

---

1. Two recent books addressing this dilemma are *How Does Analysis Cure?* (Kohut 1984) and *How Psychotherapy Works* (Weiss 1993).

TWO-PERSON PSYCHOLOGY

When I worked in a classical, one-person psychology model, I understood transference feelings—the ways in which patients experienced me—as arising from forces solely within the patients. I believed that I was neutral, even-handed, and unknown, and that my patients' experiences of me were distortions based on projections, which I interpreted.

Working in a two-person model, I view patients' feelings as determined by their past experiences and by current perceptions of me. Patients pick up cues from behaviors and attitudes that I do not always intend or realize.

An example of this is Mary, a 28-year-old depressed woman with a history of molestation by her brother and stepfather. She left a therapist four years earlier when he tried to seduce her, and she expected me to "blame" her for her "masochistic" behavior and to hold her responsible for being molested. When I did not, she felt safe, and as she felt understood, her depression lifted.

Then, after six months, her mood changed from eagerness to see me to dread of the sessions. Her comfort in being with me changed to restless agitation. "I hate coming here!" she would announce. "I can't stand these sessions. There is no point in continuing. I'm getting worse instead of better."

Anything I said was of no benefit and even upset her further. I felt helpless and guilty, and so, as is my wont, I tried harder. She felt patronized and said I was just using her, pressuring her to talk about painful experiences and causing her to feel humiliated. I felt misunderstood and unappreciated and became irritated with her. I, too, began to dread the sessions. She complained either that I wanted her to change into what I expected or that I was aloof and indifferent and didn't care if she changed at all.

I felt stuck and in a no-win position, and thought of interpretations I might have made in the past. I could point out that she was feeling frightened at the increasing closeness in our relationship, and resisting being involved with me, but this could make her feel inadequate and defeated. I could point out that she was struggling with feelings of anger toward me that were a displacement from the past, but I knew that would make her feel hurt and criticized. I could point out the distortions in her perceptions of me, but that would make her feel discounted, as she did with her mother. This way of thinking, while accurate at some level, was not central to her experience, and is a one-person psychology model, which puts the essence of the difficulty solely within her.

Winnicott (1960a), defining a two-person model, said there is no such thing as an infant, explaining that there can only be an infant and maternal care. Applying this to psychoanalysis, there is no such thing as a patient; there can only be a patient–analyst dyad. The patient's experience of me may be determined by early experiences, but these reactions are precipitated by some current perception of me.

Since this perception is codetermined by her past experiences and her present perception of my behavior, I wanted to find out what I did that set Mary off before looking at the contributions from her past. I systematically explored my contributions to her transference reactions of agitation and fear. Each time she felt upset with me, I observed that there was more tension and distance between us, and I asked her to help me understand what had happened. Could she remember what I had said that was patronizing, critical, pressuring, or discounting? I would then listen very carefully, trying to see her perspective until I could say, "Yes, now that I hear my words coming back to me, they do sound patronizing. It's no wonder you feel hurt and angry, and I appreciate your bringing it to my attention."

I did not apologize for what I said, but tried to appreciate the impact my words had on her. Her reactions to me were precipitated in some way by her perceptions of me, and although from my point of view her perceptions may have been distorted, I wanted to see her reality. I did not have to agree or disagree with her; I just had to understand her.

When she felt taken seriously, she became calm and settled, and then became sad, telling me she had overreacted. My seeing things from her perspective helped bridge a gap between us, enabling her to see things from my perspective without having to be compliant. After much repetition of this interaction, she realized that her reactions to me were familiar, and she spontaneously recalled new memories of being hurt, humiliated, patronized, and demeaned by her parents and her brothers whenever she did not comply with their expectations.

In a two-person psychology model, the patient's complaints are given first priority. The impact of this shift in theory is described by Merton Gill (1984):

> The shift from a view of transference as a distortion . . . to initial emphasis on the analyst's contribution to the transference, alters . . . the atmosphere of an analysis . . . from the patient being wrong and misguided to one in which his point of view is given initial consideration. . . . [The patient's] rational capacity is respected rather than belittled. [This] position is . . . contrary to the one which argues that to acknowledge the rationality of the patient's point of view is to confirm his belief that his experience is fully accounted for by the current behavior of the analyst. [p. 173]

The patient's transference reactions, no matter how distorted, are seen as codetermined by both early experiences and the current experience with the analyst (Stolorow and Lachmann 1980).

MOTIVATION AND RESISTANCE

When I worked in a classical mode, I understood resistance as patients running away from themselves and me. Motivated by conflicts over innate aggressive and incestuous strivings, patients did not want to be made uncomfortable by becoming aware of their unconscious wishes to confound or defeat me.

From this viewpoint, my interpretations were confrontational and authoritative. For example, John, a man in his mid-thirties, would, from time to time, point out my shortcomings. I understood and interpreted these criticisms of me as expressions of underlying anger stemming from an unconscious aggressive drive. I believed he was unconsciously hostile and competitive toward me, an expression of his Oedipus complex, a normal phase of development. John acquiesced to these interpretations and felt guilty, like a naughty child, and his already poor self-esteem deteriorated. I saw his acquiescence as confirmation of my theory.

From the perspective of self psychology I came to see patients not as striving to defeat me but as striving to grow, develop, and protect themselves. I changed my approach.

Two years later, John began a session with the statement, "I see that you wear a gold chain. I think that's really tacky!" He then began putting himself down for being so "angry." I thought he might be putting himself down in anticipation of my interpretation of his anger, his way of protecting himself from my critical interpretations, so I asked him if that seemed like anger. He said, "It sure sounds like anger to me. Doesn't it sound like anger to you?" I said that it did not feel like anger to me, but sounded as if he was trying, somewhat awkwardly, to express his own opinion, to pursue some of his own ideas. I saw his assertiveness as a reaction to feelings of enmeshment with me and an attempt to resume his individuation.

Reframing his behavior had a powerful impact on the analysis. He was no longer a naughty boy being obnoxious, but was, instead, a frightened man struggling to find his voice. When I had seen him as angry at me, he felt criticized and frightened of losing me. He believed that if we became disconnected, he would lose all the gains of his analysis. He had to comply, to "kow-tow" in order to maintain my support, and this made him feel enslaved and humiliated. He was torn between being his own person and keeping me happy, and did not believe he could do both, or that he had a right to develop as an independent

person. As this new understanding became conscious, his individuation resumed its course with an improvement in self-
cohesion and self-esteem.

While working in a traditional model, I viewed his anger as
a manifestation of aggressive drive energy directed at me, but
from the perspective of self psychology, I saw his anger as
assertiveness in the service of self-individuation development
(Mahler et al. 1975). These changes in understanding have
modified my attitude toward patients and my interpretations
of their responses.

Self psychology has influenced our theory of normal development. Kohut (1982) objected to the traditional psychoanalytic
view that people are motivated primarily by inborn, unconscious
drives, aggressive and incestuous strivings needing to be tamed.
He said that ". . . we are dealing with drive experiences and not
with drives" (1984, p. 208). In Kohut's view, our innate strivings
are toward growth and development. "Self psychology believes
that man's essence is . . . to realize the program laid down in
his depth during the span of his life" (Kohut 1982, p. 402).

In talking to patients, analysts informed by traditional theory
will look for, and systematically point out, the distortions and
projections that derive from aggressive and incestuous strivings.
Analysts informed by self psychology will, by contrast, see
aggressive and incestuous strivings as symptomatic of blocks
in development. The patient who envies and wants to destroy
the analyst's power is not acting out a natural, inborn, instinctual urge, but is, instead, frustrated, overwhelmed, and valiantly
fighting to overcome feelings of fragmentation or disruption. The
analytic goal here is to understand and remove what blocks this
patient from feeling more organized, so that the developmental process toward self-cohesion can resume its natural course.
Shane (1979) says that "developmental progression may be as
significant to the process of analysis as interpretations and insight itself" (p. 375).

Kohut (1977) also disagreed with Freud's idea that the Oedipus complex is a part of normal development. Later he differ-

entiates the normal and joyful oedipal phase from abnormal
oedipal anxieties, explaining that

> . . . the healthy child of healthy parents enters the oedipal
> phase joyfully. The joy he experiences is due not only to
> the fact that he himself responds with pride to a develop-
> mental achievement, that is, to a new and expanding capa-
> city for affection and assertiveness, but also to the fact that
> this achievement elicits a glow of empathic joy and pride
> from the side of the oedipal-phase selfobjects. Owing to this
> joy and pride of achievement, the boy's affectionate atti-
> tude does not disintegrate into fragmented sexual im-
> pulses, his assertiveness is not transformed into destruc-
> tive hostility, and he is not intensely afraid of his parents.
> Only if his parents do not function appropriately as oedi-
> pal selfobjects will the child experience high degrees of
> anxiety. [Kohut 1984, p. 14]

The oedipal aggressive and incestuous strivings that we see
in patients are reactions to injury. For example, a small boy will
look to his father for help in developing normal assertiveness,
and if the father takes pride and shows pleasure in his son's
healthy assertiveness, the boy will not feel conflict. If, however,
the father feels threatened by his son's assertiveness and reacts
with anger, disapproval, and contempt, his son will feel hurt,
angry, and humiliated. This tension is the cause of the irrational guilt and competitive rage previously thought to be a part
of normal development, and

> . . . the normal oedipal self that should be a center of inde-
> pendent affectionate and assertive initiative will break into
> fragments and become weakened and disharmonious if its
> affection and assertiveness do not elicit the parents' proud
> mirroring responses . . . but eventuate instead in the par-
> ents . . . stimulation and . . . hostile competitiveness. [Kohut
> 1984, p. 24]

Incestuous tensions also are a reaction to injury. Children normally are intensely passionate, and if a mother takes pride in her son's love for her, the little boy will not feel conflict. If, however, his mother feels unhappy in her personal life and turns to the boy with a seductive attitude, he will feel sexually stimulated and conflicted, like a child who is molested. If this seductive mother otherwise ignores him, and his father is distant or absent, he may experience incestuous strivings as his only avenue to a human connection.

In normal development, a father will take pride in his son's developing sexuality, but if the father feels competitive with his son, the boy's affection for his mother will make the father anxious. If the father also withdraws from his son, the boy may feel more isolated and anxious, and forced to rely on erotic feelings for comfort.

Kohut (1984) states:

> . . . the girl's *primary* oedipal fears are of being confronted by a nonempathically sexually seductive rather than affection-accepting paternal selfobject or by a competitive-hostile rather than pridefully pleased maternal one. The boy's primary oedipal fears, on the other hand, are of being confronted by a nonempathic sexually seductive rather than affection-accepting maternal selfobject or by a competitive-hostile rather than pridefully pleased paternal one. [p. 24]

Kohut goes on to state that *pathological sexual drivenness* and *destructive hostility* arise secondary to experiences of *fragmentation or enfeeblement* of the self.

When oedipal anxieties arise in the transference, we no longer accept them as the inevitable expression of normal development, but, instead, investigate and understand the injuries, including those at the hands of the analyst, that generate these anxieties.

3

The Role of
Psychoanalysis

My role in society, or any artist or poet's role, is to try and express what we all feel. Not to tell people how to feel. Not as a preacher, not as a leader, but as a reflection of us all.
John Lennon

Does psychoanalysis have a viable role in the current health care climate? With the advent of managed care and the proliferation of new therapies aimed at rapid cure and low cost, analytic therapists are in the minority, and the cost of their services excludes them from most insurance plans. Yet a steady stream of individuals finds psychoanalysis the treatment of choice. These people are willing to invest in analysis, which is as essential to them as having a car. Some are therapists who, overwhelmed by the stress of their practices and the needs of their patients, turn for help to those outside of managed care, those with the best training to help them understand themselves and their patients. Others have tried short-term therapies and found they needed more.

Psychoanalysis does indeed have a vital place in the therapeutic community, especially for people like Adam, a 35-year-old successful business man, happily married, with young children, who felt something was lacking in his life. Although he loved his wife and children, he felt empty inside and was reserved in his relationships. Buying a new car or taking a trip always provided a spark of excitement that relieved the empty feeling, but as soon as the novelty wore off, or he returned to his routine, the empty feeling returned. The feeling of emptiness and his reserved behavior occurred automatically despite Adam's conscious efforts to change. He found relief by impulsively spending money, but then he got behind financially and had to work harder.

Over time, a variety of individual and group psychotherapies helped, but he could not shake off a feeling of detachment, and could not break through the wall between himself and his wife and children. He decided to try psychoanalysis, went five times a week for four years, and discovered hidden forces operating within him. He realized that unconscious feelings of vulnerability set in motion self-protective mechanisms, particularly at times of intimacy. For example, if his son wanted a story read to him, Adam would agree and then suddenly remember an unfinished business project that needed his attention. These self-protective mechanisms happened without conscious awareness.

In his analysis, he developed a reflective self-awareness, and he wondered about the origins of these automatic behaviors. Analytic exploration led to previously forgotten memories of painful early experiences with his parents, who fought openly and bitterly. Adam had not realized how responsible he felt for their fighting. He believed it was a reflection of his inadequacy as a son.

His mother belittled his father, who retreated to watching television and drinking beer. Occasionally his father took young Adam to the tavern, where he bragged about him. Adam loved this special time with his father, but the spell was broken as his mother launched into a tirade criticizing his father for corrupting her son when they returned home. Adam felt crushed and frightened by his mother's outbursts toward his father. He believed that closeness with his father hurt his mother, and he withdrew from his father to protect his mother.

Mother reacted to her husband's withdrawal and her son's isolation by lavishing attention on her son. Adam basked in her love, but soon became aware that she was proud of him only when he stayed close to her and relied on her, when he made her feel needed. If he behaved independently or was self-sufficient, he saw a hurt look in her eyes and sensed a sudden coolness from her. He could stay close to her only by giving up his budding individuality. He could pursue his own path and protect himself from enmeshment with her neediness only by maintaining a reserve, a discreet emotional distance.

These early ways of relating developed into unconscious patterns, into habitual ways of relating to people, that now shaped his experiences with his wife and his children. The gradual unfolding and illumination of these patterns in the analysis made possible the development of new patterns of organizing principles (Stolorow and Atwood 1992). As the underlying feelings of vulnerability came into awareness and were understood, new feelings of strength and confidence emerged and new experiences of intimacy developed.

Adam felt happier in his relationships, and his new confidence resulted in increased productivity at work and a marked decrease in his impulsive spending. Adam found that in addition to improving his relationships, his analysis was a good investment.

PSYCHOANALYSIS AND TRANSFERENCE

I want to clarify how I use the terms *psychoanalysis*, *transference*, and *countertransference*, terms that have little uniformity or agreement among psychoanalysts. Psychoanalysis is taught in psychoanalytic institutes and practiced by graduates of those institutes. Traditionally, psychoanalysis is defined as a therapeutic method that, through the analysis of the transference, eliminates defenses and resistances and enriches the personality (Moore and Fine 1968), but the meanings of *transference* and *analysis of the transference* are subject to much debate, as is the concept of *countertransference*.

Traditionally, transference is defined as those feelings displaced from the past and projected in distorted fashion onto the analyst. Countertransference is defined as feelings from the analyst's past stirred up by the patient's transference reactions and projected onto the patient. Patients in analysis come to experience their analysts in ways that are similar to important past relationships, and analysts similarly come to experience their patients as they did important figures from their pasts.

These terms have taken on new meanings as "major changes in technical emphasis brought about the extension, the stretching of a concept such as transference, so that it came to include a variety of object-related activities which need not be repetitions of relationships to important figures in the past" (Sandler 1983, p. 41). This stretching, Sandler points out, has led to disagreements, but "without disagreement psychoanalytic theory would be dead" (p. 41).

My view of transference and of countertransference continues to change. At present, I view transference as the patient's habitual way of organizing his or her experience of a relationship, including all the emotional feelings experienced by the patient toward the therapist (Stolorow and Lachmann 1984–1985). I think of countertransference as all the ways in which the analyst experiences the patient (Fosshage 1994).

PSYCHOANALYSIS AND PSYCHOTHERAPY

Defining psychoanalysis and differentiating it from psychoanalytic psychotherapy is more difficult, even for a distinguished panel at the 1953 meeting of the American Psychoanalytic Association who could not agree on an acceptable definition of these therapies (Rangell 1954). Psychoanalysis originally referred to a therapy where analysis of the transference was central, and psychotherapy was where the transference was manipulated rather than analyzed. As psychotherapists began getting supervision from psychoanalysts, however, they too began analyzing the transference and adopting analytic techniques in once- and twice-weekly therapy. The distinctions between psychotherapy and psychoanalysis became blurred.

My definition of psychoanalysis is in two parts: first that psychoanalysis is a therapy practiced by someone who is psychoanalytically trained, and second, the part influenced by Gill, that psychoanalysis is a therapy based on the systematic investigation of the analyst's contributions to the patient's transference reactions. By systematic investigation, I mean that the analyst looks first at his or her contributions before looking at contributions from past relationships or other current relationships.

In distinguishing psychoanalysis from psychotherapy, Gill (1984) comes to the conclusion that "the centrality of the analysis of transference, as I have defined transference, the refusal to manipulate it, and the searching out and making explicit whatever one can discern of inadvertent manipulation of the transference is alone the distinguishing characteristic of analytic technique" (p. 172). From this perspective, many who believe they are practicing psychoanalysis are doing psychotherapy, and many who believe they are doing psychotherapy are practicing psychoanalysis.

I believe that a psychoanalyst is always practicing psychoanalysis whether seeing someone once a week, once a month or every day. I have supervised cases from social agencies where patients seen once a month over a ten-year period developed, investigated, and resolved intense transferences resulting in significant personality development and change.

While managed care and short-term therapies have increased the number of patients seeking help, they have not decreased the number of people seeking long-term help. Psychoanalysis, its obituary written many times, continues to thrive and flourish, and its practitioners continue to be in demand as teachers, supervisors, and therapists.

4

Mode of Investigation

Happy the man who could search out the causes of things.
Virgil

Kohut (1959) set in motion a quiet revolution, self psychology, when he described the empathic-introspective mode of investigation. Prior to this paradigm, traditional psychoanalytic technique centered around the interpretation of resistance and defense. Defenses, in this model, are unconscious mechanisms set up to protect against forbidden instinctual wishes; resistances are attempts by the patient to oppose the analyst and the analysis.

TRADITIONAL PSYCHOANALYTIC TECHNIQUE

Traditional psychoanalytic technique is described by Greenson (1967):

The most important analytic procedure is *interpretation*; all others are subordinated to it . . . The term "analyzing" is a short hand expression which refers to those insight-furthering techniques. It usually includes four distinct procedures: *confrontation*, *clarification*, *interpretation*, and *working through*. [p. 37]

Greenson continues: "The first step in analyzing a psychic phenomenon is *confrontation*. The phenomenon in question has to be made evident, has to be made explicit to the patient's conscious ego" (pp. 37–38). He then defines interpretation as making "an unconscious phenomenon conscious" (p. 39), and working through, he says, "refers . . . to the repetitive, progressive, and elaborate explorations of the resistances which prevent an insight from leading to change" (p.42). Greenson views confrontation and interpretation in an authoritarian way: the analyst has to make evident or make explicit some phenomenon to the patient.

THE EMPATHIC-INTROSPECTIVE MODE AND TECHNIQUE

Lichtenberg and colleagues (1992) state: "An inherent contradiction exists between the empathic mode of perception and the traditional treatment of defenses by confrontation and interpretation" (p. 153). The empathic-introspective mode views defense and resistance differently. In this model, defense and resistance are a person's normal attempts at self-protection when anticipating pain or injury. The analyst assumes that the patient has valid reasons for resisting the analyst or the analysis, and wants to understand, from the patient's perspective, what he or she fears, and what, if anything, the analyst contributes to that fear.

Kohut (1959) defined the empathic-introspective mode of investigation, the understanding of material, from the patient's vantage point. Using the concept of *oral dependence* as an illustration of the difference between the two models, he said that repressed dependency strivings found in adult analysands traditionally are considered to represent the mental state of the infant nursing at the breast. He continued:

> In order to demonstrate the unreliability of such efforts, we may entertain the opposite hypothesis and claim that rudimentary self-awareness of the healthy infant at the

breast should rather be compared with the emotional state of an adult who is totally absorbed in an activity of the utmost importance to him as, for example, the sprinter at the last few yards of the 100-yard dash, the virtuoso at the height of the cadenza, or the lover at the peak of sexual union. The assumption, that dependence states in the adult are a reversion to a primal psychological gestalt that cannot be further reduced by analysis, is, thus, opposed by our empathic understanding of healthy children. [p. 474]

Kohut goes on to state that reactions of clinging dependence in adults are not a representation of the mental state of healthy children. They are instead, he says, an expression of childhood pathology, such as reactions to experiences of rejection.

Lawrence Friedman (1988), describing the impact of this revolution, said,

It must be an impressive experience for a patient to have his pathology consistently given its progressive rather that its regressive significance—to be told that his immaturity is not a hammock but a launching pad, his incompleteness a purple heart from deprivation, not a badge of indolence, greed and cowardice. [p. 385]

A clinical example of working in the empathic-introspective mode is given by Malin (1993) who describes his patient, Mr. G, who insisted, two years into the analysis, that Malin remain absolutely silent for four months. Malin initially saw the request as a resistance (in the traditional sense), and dealt with it interpretively. The patient felt criticized, and the therapeutic connection was disrupted. Then Malin understood the request, from the patient's perspective, as a developmental need requiring patience and understanding. "After several more sessions of exploring this persistent demand, at two years and three months into the analysis, I agreed to saying nothing except to indicate when our time was up, which Mr. G accepted as necessary. My absolute silence continued for over four months," said Malin (p. 512). The disruption was repaired, and the patient did much productive analytic work. By staying with his patient's experience, at times with much turmoil, great progress was made. Malin says, "My willingness to acknowledge Mr. G's point of view . . . seemed crucial to the eventual therapeutic result" (p. 517).

When patients feel understood, they become stronger and more insightful. Their analysts, by focusing on understanding their patients' experiences, feel unburdened from the pressures to ferret out and confront unconscious motives. Self psychologists take exception to confrontation because it implies defiance and is used traditionally to analyze from an unempathic, authoritarian perspective. The analyst's reality is imposed on the patient. Confrontation, however, can also mean "to bring together for examination or comparison," a definition more compatible with self psychology.

THE EMPATHIC-INTROSPECTIVE MODE AND CONFRONTATIONS

A common misunderstanding of self psychology is that the empathic-introspective mode means that one avoids interpretation of psychic conflict (Lachmann 1986) and only stays with a patient's experience (Trop 1994). There are times, however, when staying exclusively with the patient's experience is not helpful or empathic. Times will arise when the analyst will need to confront the patient, to ask the patient to understand the analyst's view of what the patient presents. An example of such a confrontation is one in which Kohut (1984), instead of sympathetically understanding his patient's frustration and irritation, wanted to express concern about the patient's behavior. The patient was behaving arrogantly and dangerously, and Kohut said to him, "You are a complete idiot" (p. 74).

The following is an example where I first used the empathic-introspective mode by staying exclusively with a patient's experience to achieve understanding, and then used the empathic-introspective mode by stepping outside the patient's viewpoint to share my experience. Bennett, a 38-year-old attorney, began his analysis with complaints each day that I never said good morning to him. I knew I said good morning, but I wanted to stay with his experience and not confront what I perceived as his distortion. Each day, accommodating myself to his point of view, I tried saying good morning a little louder, but he continued to lament, "It drives me crazy that you never say good morning when I come in."

I felt like telling him, "I said good morning! Didn't you hear me?" I wondered to myself, "Does he have some unconscious need to disavow my greeting, to keep me at a distance?" I knew that was accurate at a deeper level, but it was early in the analysis and I believed that staying with his experience would be productive.

I then wondered if there could be some subjective truth encoded in his perception of me. I explored how it made Bennett feel when he came in each morning and did not experience a greeting from me. "It feels awful. It reminds me of when I was little and waited each morning outside my father's room for hours until he would get up and come out," he said. His father worked late and slept late. He was depressed and stayed isolated in his room for hours. When he finally emerged, he showed no eagerness to see Bennett. The little boy looked in vain for some spark, some sign of recognition, only to be disappointed.

I realized that because we met at an early hour I was not fully awake when I greeted him. Although I said good morning, there was no spark of pleasure or excitement in my greeting. Exploring the impact of my lack of enthusiasm revealed that not only was he disappointed, he also felt ashamed. He had believed that his father's lack of response was his fault, was his failure as a son. After recalling and talking about his feelings of shame and failure, he was able to see things from my vantage point, acknowledge my greeting, and say good morning to me in return.

Two years later, my stance of staying only with his experience led to a therapeutic impasse and a real-life crisis. Bennett

was getting into trouble with superiors for being late to important meetings and then leaving early. He felt helpless in the face
of his superiors' lack of understanding. I doggedly stayed with
his experience, appreciating how frustrating and discouraging
it was for him to have self-centered superiors who did not understand his needs. I expected that feeling allied with me, he would
eventually see spontaneously, from his employer's vantage
point, that his behavior was provocative.

Bennett's situation at work deteriorated further; he still did
not recognize his contribution to the problem, and I became concerned. I felt frustrated and at an impasse; my stance of staying with his experience was not working. I realized I was being
sympathetic, not empathic. As a result, I changed tack and confronted him with my understanding of his contribution. I asked,
"Didn't you realize that going in late and leaving early would
be provocative?" "No," he said thoughtfully, "but I should have!
Why didn't I realize it?" he asked. "Why didn't you warn me?"
he demanded.

Exploring his feelings, I realized that he felt vulnerable, confused, and desperately in need of a strong, protective father.
Getting back in tune with his needs, I understood that he looked
to me to be strong, to confront and protect him. I made this interpretation, and he said, "Now you understand me, but I had to
shoot myself in the foot first." He felt understood, the analytic
impasse resolved, and new memories emerged about his father's
helplessness and passivity in the face of his mother's seductive-
ness and intrusiveness.

Staying exclusively with Bennett's experience at this point
was not empathic or understanding of his need. It made him
feel that I was weak, and he became anxious. His getting into
trouble was a signal of vulnerability, a demonstration of a long-
ing to mobilize strength in others to protect him. His organizing principle, learned in early childhood, was that he had to
either hurt himself or engage in an adversarial experience before he could get help.

Illumination of these themes led to new memories of early school difficulties. Once, when a teacher understood his vulnerability and responded with interest and helpfulness, his school work improved dramatically, but another time, the teacher misunderstood, saw him as a troublemaker, and called his mother to school. His mother felt overwhelmed and acted helplessly in front of the teacher. Bennett was mortified. Like pieces of a puzzle falling into place, his experience now made sense.

With this patient, staying with his experience initially was productive. It helped him feel allied with me, and he spontaneously saw things from the vantage point of others. However, two years later, my staying only with his experience became counterproductive. Confusing sympathy with empathy, I lost touch with his needs. I had made staying with his experience into a rule, had ignored my intuition and, as a result, I was no longer empathically attuned. When I became concerned, trusted my intuition, and confronted the issue from my point of view, the empathic connection was re-established and the analytic process resumed. This time it was questioning and confronting the patient that made him feel understood. Questioning and confronting became the mode of empathic inquiry, and feeling more comfortable with my intuition and spontaneity freed me up, too.

5

Selfobject
Theory

Bore, n. A person who talks when you wish him to listen.
Ambrose Bierce

For years I felt that my job was to know what to say to patients. Patients would start a session with something in mind. I listened and tried to understand how their talking related to their present life, to their relationship with me, and to their past. At some point I felt I should share what I understood with them.

Some patients, however, did not want me to interrupt them. Instead of appreciating my insightful comments, they felt I was intruding. They politely let me finish talking, and then, ignoring my comments, resumed what they were saying. I would feel frustrated and irritated. I did not realize that many times my listening in an understanding way was more important than my talking.

Patients sometimes come to a session feeling disorganized, and talking to me is an organizing experience for them. At these times they need me to listen and to understand. If I limit myself to comments indicating my understanding they feel connected and organized, but if I go beyond their immediate experience, and try to expand their understanding, to talk about their relationship with me or something in their past, they feel disconnected and anxious. If I can allow myself to be used to provide this organizing experience, what Kohut (1971) called a *selfobject experience*, the analysis progresses. Eventually these patients begin to feel stronger and better organized, and they are able to expand their understanding to other relationships, both present and past. The analysis can proceed.

SELFOBJECT EXPERIENCES AND OBJECT EXPERIENCES

Kohut revolutionized psychoanalytic practice with his discovery of the selfobject dimension of relationships. Nothing has caused more confusion in self psychology than the term *self-object*. Much confusion can be avoided by using the term as an adjective as in *selfobject experience* or *selfobject function* instead of using it as a noun.

Selfobject experiences and object experiences are two dimensions of relating that occur simultaneously in every relationship, and have a foreground-background relationship. At any given moment in a person's experience, one of the two dimensions of relating is more in the foreground. In the object experience dimension of a relationship, the other person is experienced as a separate person, but in the selfobject experience dimension of a relationship, the other person is experienced, at that moment, as an extension of the self, like an arm or a leg. To some degree, both dimensions of relating are experienced in all relationships.

Selfobject experiences include feeling soothed, comforted, reassured, strengthened, validated, or acknowledged by another. Take soothing as an example. The ability to self-soothe varies from person to person depending on early experiences and on inborn temperament. Yet, no matter how competent you are at self-soothing, there will be times when you will be unable to provide this for yourself and you will need to turn to someone else for soothing or comforting. The person you turn to is experienced at those moments as an extension of yourself. Anyone who can furnish this soothing experience will be serving a selfobject function and offering you something you cannot provide for yourself at that moment.

This important insight sheds much light on those unpleasant experiences when we feel we are being treated like an impersonal or inanimate object. It helps us understand why our disappointment, when we are looking for a selfobject experience, feels like a betrayal. When the selfobject dimension of a relationship is more in the background, soothing experiences will feel mutual, but when the object dimension recedes into the background, as in cases of desperate vulnerability, the person supplying the soothing experience will be interchangeable with anyone who can provide that function. The experience does not feel personal or special.

SELFOBJECT EXPERIENCES IN NORMAL DEVELOPMENT

The normal state of infancy is helplessness and vulnerability. Yet small children feel strong and confident as long as they feel a tie to a parental figure. The adult offers a strengthening selfobject function for these children who are not yet able to provide it for themselves. When this strengthening tie to the adult is disrupted, however, the child will feel helpless and vulnerable.

In normal development, when adults can furnish a sufficient amount of strength and protection, children will gradually develop internal feelings of strength and competence. When adults, however, are not able to provide a protective environment, and children are repeatedly overwhelmed by feelings of vulnerability, the development of an internal sense of strength and confidence is stunted. Deprived of strengthening selfobject figures, these children grow up feeling vulnerable and in desperate need of ties to strong figures to maintain normal self-cohesion.

Another developmental arrest commonly occurs when children begin to create and use imagination. A little boy collects some rocks and proudly presents them to his mother as a gift. When his mother beams with enthusiasm, and says, "Oh, you brought me precious jewels—they're beautiful," the little boy glows with pride. His mother's pleasure gives him a validating, selfobject experience, and he feels an internal sense of accomplishment and goodness.

However, if his mother does not beam with pleasure, but reacts with horror and disgust, exclaiming, "Oh, those rocks are filthy. Get them out of the house!" the little boy feels ashamed. His attempt at initiative has translated into a sense of failure and incompetence.

If a little girl gets dressed up, runs to her father, and beams at him, and her father mirrors back her pride with the response, "Oh, you look beautiful, so grown up!" his daughter glows with pleasure. She feels proud of her appearance. If the father, however, limits his comments to finding her faults, remarking that, "The bow in your hair is crooked," or "There is a hole in your stocking," the little girl feels crushed, humiliated, and ashamed of herself.

When parents can provide a sufficient amount of mirroring and validating selfobject responses, children develop pride in their achievements and feel a sense of competence, but when children are continually deprived of these essential selfobject responses, this aspect of their development is stunted. They feel an internal sense of deficiency, inadequacy, and shame. They go through life needing continual external validation and acknowledgment to feel good about themselves.

The need for selfobject experiences is normal and is present throughout life. One never outgrows this need. When our expectations are met, we feel good; when disappointed, we feel tension. What determines pathology is not the need for selfobject experiences, but the degree of difficulty in dealing with selfobject failures.

Relatively cohesive individuals with a stable self-structure will handle disappointments by falling back on inner resources to deal with the resulting state of tension. Individuals who feel deficient, however, and unable to trust their inner resources, who lack confidence in their ability to judge what is best, will react to disappointments with varying degrees of disruption. Disruptions, at their worst, may take the form of panic, rage, or extreme withdrawal. Attempts to repair feelings of disruption can include impulsive behavior, drug use, eating disorders, sexual perversions, or self-mutilation.

Kohut (1984) took issue with the "maturity-morality" inherent in psychoanalytic theories. In traditional theory dependency needs are viewed as regression or as a lack of maturity. The goal of traditional psychoanalysis is autonomy. The goal of therapy, in this model, is not to achieve independence (to not need anybody), but to be able to deal with frustrations and disappointments without fragmentation or loss of cohesion.

SELFOBJECT EXPERIENCES
AND TRANSFERENCE

In psychoanalysis, both selfobject and object dimensions of relating will be experienced in the transference, in the selfobject dimension of transference where the patient feels safe and understood, and in the object or repetitive dimension of transference where the patient experiences both intimacy and conflict with the analyst (Stolorow and Lachmann 1984–1985). Phase-appropriate developmental needs, such as affirmation, validation, and idealization, are revived in the selfobject dimension of the transference, and represent attempts to "resume a thwarted development" (Ornstein 1991, p. 381).

The following is an example in which I was experienced by a patient as providing two different, impersonal selfobject functions. The patient, a 32-year-old bright, attractive woman, had accomplished her goal of getting married and starting a family. She entered analysis because, although not feeling particularly depressed, her life seemed dull, empty, and meaningless. She had devoted herself to her husband and child, and resented that they did not reciprocate and devote themselves equally to her. Her husband had many outside activities, but she had no time for them. She complained bitterly about his lack of attention, and worried about her inability to stay on a diet and her habit of biting her nails. In the analysis she reported every frustration, hour after hour, with little emotional feeling.

Her father died when she was a child, and although she recalled many painful memories, she never cried. Over the years she made slow but steady progress in the analysis. She developed object transferences where she experienced repetitions of traumatic early experiences, including feeling judged and criticized by me, feeling pressured by me to perform, and feeling that I was disappointed in her. As these transference feelings were worked through and resolved, she dieted and lost weight, and stopped biting her nails. She also developed time for outside activities, but pursued them without enthusiasm.

The talking, however, went on endlessly, and I often felt that she was talking at me and not to me. I came to understand that she had developed a selfobject transference, and I was being used to serve a validating or sounding board function for her. As a little girl, she had been deprived of the normal validating and acknowledging responses where she could relate her experiences and feelings, be heard and understood, and not be told to do something about it. Instead of being made to feel understood, she was made to feel that she was a troublemaker.

On occasion, when I would cancel one of our sessions to take a vacation, she would come in anyway, by mistake, and sit in my waiting room for fifteen or twenty minutes before realizing the session had been canceled. She didn't think there was anything strange about this. When I wondered if this had something to do with feelings of missing me, she would say, "Absolutely not! Why would I have any feelings about you?" She could not understand why I was so egotistical and always insisted that elements of her behavior were related to me. I was just an employee, someone she paid who performed a service, and there was nothing personal in it. When I interpreted what I saw as denial, as resistance to the negative transference, the progress stopped, and we came to an impasse.

I came to realize that at this phase of her analysis, she had developed an archaic selfobject transference where she looked to me to provide an organizing function that she could not provide for herself. There were other transferences that had developed in the course of her analysis, but here was a new facet.

When I understood this and could see from her perspective that she experienced me as providing a function for her, I was able to say, "Perhaps you missed the analysis." "Yes," she said emphatically, "now you understand. Coming here is something I do every day. If I didn't have here to come, I wouldn't know what to do with myself." She did not need to see me. All she needed at this phase was to come, to spend some time in my waiting room, and then she could feel organized enough to go out and perform the rest of her daily activities. I was reminded of the small child in the practicing subphase of separation-individuation who returns to the mother from time to time for "refueling" (Mahler et al. 1975). The mother does not have to be personally engaged; just touching her chair is enough for the child.

The patient then reported a dream in which she was swimming in a lake, holding onto a floating device, a swimming raft. In the analysis of the dream I was the swimming raft, and was performing a supporting function for her. The interpretation of this aspect of the transference led to the recall of new material and new memories about her mother's coldness and unavailability during her childhood.

Her mother had complained of feeling sick and had to stay in bed. When she was 6, she had to get her own breakfast, and her older brother had to tie the bow on the back of her dress so that she could go to school because Mother was unable to get out of bed and perform these functions. The little girl could not express her frustration and felt her mother's failure to provide support as evidence of her own inadequacy. She did not feel she had a right to expect her mother to take care of her. She should have been able to do these things for herself. She felt she did not have a right to be frustrated when she could not do these things. Her mother had told her that it was the child's complaints that made Mother sick. Although the child did a great deal for herself and was quite self-sufficient, she was told that she was not good enough.

We now understood that she was deprived of the maternal validation needed to feel pleased with her achievements, and was blocked in the development of feeling competent and confident. Because of her feelings of vulnerability, she needed to maintain her image of Mother as ideal and her image of herself as inadequate. She felt she could be strong only as long as she remained tied to a strong figure, first her husband and then me. Now she became able to see her mother's limitations, anxiety, and neediness, and her self-concept improved.

This understanding, combined with these new emotional experiences of feeling acknowledged and validated by me, led to a resolution of this block in her development. With the resumption of the developmental process she started trusting herself and started taking chances with success. Her confidence and sense of cohesiveness grew rapidly. She became able to trust her own judgment and her ability to support herself in new situations. She became less tied to her husband, and, paradoxically, closer to him. Her marriage improved. Similarly, she became less tied to me and, as she continued to feel stronger, she was able to enter the termination phase and complete her analysis. She was free to develop enthusiasm for a new career, which she successfully pursued.

When I felt and interpreted that her behavior was directed at me personally, an object experience, I distanced myself from her and caused her anxiety. When I understood her developmental need to use me to provide selfobject experiences, to be a sounding board and to provide an organizing function, I interpreted her need for the analysis and I felt closer to her. She felt understood and progress continued. Bacal (1985) says that "there is a basic tendency . . . in every individual that requires the optimal responsiveness of the selfobject in order to be realized" (p. 216). When my responsiveness was in tune with her needs, she developed her own self-organizing abilities.

SELFOBJECT EXPERIENCES AND INTUITION

Understanding the need for selfobject experiences made me rethink a supervisory experience that I had thirty years ago with Editha Sterba, a Viennese child psychoanalyst who escaped from the Nazis and emigrated to Detroit with her psychoanalyst husband Richard. She supervised my treatment of a 6-year-old girl with school phobia, an otherwise healthy and delightful child, who refused to leave her mother and go to school. After months of play therapy, of dealing with her separation anxieties, her control conflicts and her oedipal fears, she became brighter and more confident, but she still refused to go to school.

In despair, I called Editha who said, "The solution is simple. On Monday, have the father take the little girl to school." I did not understand, but I followed her instructions and, on Monday, the father took the little girl to school without incident. He took her to the school door, waved good-bye and continued on to work as the little girl went happily inside. Sterba explained, "It is not the girl who has the anxiety; it is the mother. The girl stays home to take care of the mother's anxiety." The father was not anxious, and the girl felt free to go to school.

Sterba did not have a psychoanalytic explanation for this treatment—she acted intuitively. Now I understood that the mother was using her child to take care of her own anxiety, and to provide a selfobject function for the mother. Once the father stepped in and offered the strength his daughter needed, she was able to get on with her development.

Experienced psychoanalysts have always understood intuitively the need for selfobject experiences. They lacked, however, a theoretical framework in which to teach the technique of understanding and dealing with selfobject needs. Ralph Greenson once chastised a psychoanalytic candidate for not asking his patient about her sick baby. The woman had canceled the previous session to take the child to the hospital. He was then asked, "But Dr. Greenson, is that analysis?" Greenson replied, "I don't care what you call it, that's what you do!" He understood intuitively the woman's need for acknowledgment of her pain. Self psychology has given us the theoretical framework within which we can now offer technical guidelines for talking to patients about their selfobject needs.

Many of the symptoms we see in our consulting rooms, addictions, impulsive behaviors, violent rages, obsessional preoccupations, and sexual compulsions, are most often desperate attempts at coping with feelings of disruption or emptiness, feelings secondary to unmet selfobject needs.

6

Intersubjectivity
Theory

I celebrate myself, and sing myself,
And what I assume you will assume,
For every atom belonging to me as good belongs to you.
                                                    Walt Whitman

SOLIPSISM

I entered medical school in 1954 at Wayne State University. John Dorsey, professor, psychoanalyst, and philosopher, taught beginning psychiatry. Dorsey revered both Freud, who was his analyst, and Walt Whitman, the poet. Dorsey's philosophy was solipsism: only the self exists.

"I am my own everything," Dorsey would say. He began each lecture by drawing a large circle on the blackboard with the word *me* in the center. He then drew another circle inside the first, which he called *my you*, referring to one of the students. A second *my you* circle referred to another student, and an intersecting circle referred to *my yours his*. No two students could experience another student in the same way. Each person's experience of another was subjective and unique. This was my introduction to intersubjectivity theory.

My objective-minded classmates complained that they saw no practical relevance to Dorsey's strange way of talking. Some even wondered if he was psychotic. Five years later I saw Dorsey in action when I was a resident in psychiatry, and the professor interviewed a patient in front of the staff at grand rounds.

The interns, residents, staff psychiatrists, and nurses crowded into the small conference room and sat in a semicircle around two chairs. Dorsey occupied one chair and the other was empty. The chief resident escorted in the patient, a young woman admitted to the locked ward the night before because of agitation, confusion, and delusional thinking.

Wearing a dingy hospital bathrobe, pajamas, and paper slippers, she shuffled mutely into the room, her right arm twitching, her neck jerking, and her gaze fixed on the ceiling. Reaching the chair, she slouched into it and continued looking up at the ceiling with blinking eyes. I was angry at what I saw as an attempt to embarrass the professor.

Dorsey looked at her, slouched down in his chair, looked up at the ceiling, and began to blink his eyes. After a moment he said to the chief resident, "That overhead light is very bright, do you think you could turn it down?" The resident switched off the light, plunging the room into a shadowy dimness. "That light really hurts the eyes," he said softly to the woman. She sat up in her chair, looked at Dorsey, and began talking to him, her first coherent conversation since her admission to the hospital.

Dorsey had gotten inside the woman's subjective experience and she felt the connection. It was an organizing experience for her, and she could then talk coherently. Dorsey had demonstrated the empathic-introspective mode of investigation, although he would not have called it that. For Dorsey it was intuitive—he could demonstrate it, but not teach it. Kohut gave us the vocabulary and the understanding to make the teaching possible.

PSYCHOANALYTIC PHENOMENOLOGY

Atwood and Stolorow (1979), working independently of Kohut, developed a framework for a theory of subjectivity, and they called it *psychoanalytic phenomenology*. They first used the term *intersubjective* in a paper (Stolorow, Atwood, and Ross

1978). Stolorow's work on intersubjectivity theory developed parallel with and became enriched by self psychology (Stolorow 1992).

By intersubjective, Stolorow means the psychological field formed by the reciprocal interplay between the differing subjective worlds of two (or more) individuals. What is observed clinically is conditioned, at least in part, by the observer and by the field in which the observations are made. There is no pure, objective reality. Both patient and analyst bring their subjective experiences, including their theories, to the therapy. Treatment takes place at the interface of these differing subjectivities. This interface is also a focus of analytic investigation.

Applying intersubjectivity theory to the psychoanalytic process, Stolorow and Atwood (1992) emphasize understanding the unconscious organizing principles and the developing of new organizing principles:

> Such analysis, from a position within the patient's subjective frame of reference, with the codetermining impact of the analyst on the organization of the patient's experience always kept in view, both facilitates the engagement and expansion of the patient's capacity for self-reflection and gradually establishes the analyst as an understanding presence to whom the patient's formerly invariant ordering principles must accommodate, inviting syntheses of alternative modes of experiencing self and other. [p. 34]

In other words, as patients become more reflectively aware of their unconscious processes, and have new experiences with their analysts, they develop new ways of experiencing themselves in relationships.

TECHNICAL IMPLICATIONS

Two articles in recent psychoanalytic literature demonstrate the contrasts between traditional analytic understanding and self psychology. The first article, in the *International Journal of*

Psycho-Analysis, is in an issue devoted to case presentations by psychoanalysts from differing theoretical perspectives. One presentation is by Scott L. Carder (1991) who describes himself as "nondenominational" and "influenced by Kohut and Schwaber," among others. Carder says that "Schwaber's view attempts to minimize the imposition of theory on a patient." Schwaber believes that there is a difference between an investigation that attempts to help the patient arrive at a truth, already known to the analyst, and an interpretation that investigates a question to which the analyst does not yet have an answer.

That sounded good to me, but Carder failed to implement Schwaber's ideas, to make the leap from theory to practice as is illustrated by a patient of his, a 40-year-old depressed woman, who grew up with an emotionally cold, moralistically rigid father, and a "crazy, critical, and demanding mother." Her difficulties in intimacy were interpreted by the analyst, in traditional fashion, as due to conflicts over sexual desires for her father and guilt over those desires. Her resistances were seen by Carder as arising from forces solely within her, and not from within an intersubjective matrix.

His interpretations led to a change from an idealized transference to a sexualized transference. The patient then reported a dream:

> I was in bed with my uncle Tom. . . . We embraced and I had no pubic hair. . . . It was like I was a little girl again. . . . it was understood there would be no intercourse. . . . He became turned on and was going to have sex. I said no and threatened, and then did call to my father, who came and Tom had to stop. We were both naked from the waist down. Father saw Tom and asked why he was naked. I tried to hide myself, to cover my rear with a shirt and had a cover in front of me so Daddy would not see my bare rear and know I was naked too. It didn't work. He saw and asked me why I was naked. He was accusing me. I told him I was innocent or I wouldn't have called him. [pp. 388–389]

The analyst understood this dream as her seducing the uncle (analyst) into wanting her as an expression of her oedipal desire, guilt, and fear. He interpreted that she wanted to turn him on and when she couldn't get what she wanted she called to her father/husband and tried to cover her rear so he would think she was innocent. Carder discounted the patient's statement, "I was innocent." He, the authority, knew better, and had taken a traditional approach.

He did not explore her experience, her perception of the analyst. From the empathic-introspective mode, one would wonder if she had noticed anything to suggest that he might be critical of her longings, or if he contributed in any way to her feeling turned on or her need to cover up. Did she, perhaps, see him as turned on? Carder did not explore the meanings of her sexual longings, and assumed, from a traditional perspective, that they were just oedipal strivings. He did not consider, from an empathic-introspective mode for example, that the erotic longings might be a desperate attempt by a little girl to connect with another human being in a cold, empty environment.

A self psychologically informed psychoanalyst would wonder if her compliance and humiliation were the price she felt she had to pay in childhood to maintain a vital tie with parental figures, and if that traumatic experience was now being relived with her analyst. Could she now be feeling that she has to comply with the analyst's theories to maintain her tie with him? The impact of the analyst and the analyst's theories is a central focus of investigation in intersubjectivity theory.

In the second article, from an issue of *Psychoanalytic Inquiry*, Homer Curtis (1990), a traditional analyst, gives an example of modern, classical psychoanalytic thinking. He is discussing a case presentation by James Fosshage (1990), a self psychologist. The case presented is a 28-year-old woman who became depressed during a previous analysis and left her analyst after three years. In the analysis with Fosshage, she reported feeling emotionally abandoned by her mother and remembered being hospitalized at age 3 for an unknown physical illness.

Mother did not visit her for three days. Curtis criticizes Fosshage for not considering the patient's projections and for not pursuing the patient's contributions to the early traumatic experiences. He states:

> The patient's memory . . . at age three may be useful. Here . . . we may be in a position to expand our view if we consider the possibility of screen-memory formation. . . . While accepting and working with the psychic "truth" represented in the remembered and the manifest experience, our psychoanalytic approach must consider the additional and latent meanings. . . . in the case of this memory, our curiosity should be aroused by several interesting signals. . . . How much can we take at face value a memory from age three? And for that matter, how does the patient know she was age three? Is this derived from documented fact, family stories, home movies or pictures? And what about all those threes: age three; three days before mother came; in Friday's dream her sister's deathlike sleep for three days; and an analytic schedule of three sessions a week into the third year of analysis? All this without drawing on three as a phallic or Oedipal symbol! [pp. 500–501]

In this traditional view, patients are not trusted; the analyst is the authority. Bernard Brandchaft, a self psychologist, once said that patients who do not feel good about themselves will not feel better about themselves when they experience their analysts as continually pointing out their shortcomings.

CASE ILLUSTRATION

Belle, a 19-year-old woman, had been through the system. Diagnosed as schizophrenic and labeled as untreatable, she was referred to a chronic care facility when a colleague asked me to see her. He was a friend of Belle's family and had not seen her professionally. "I don't know what's wrong with her," he said, "but I can't believe she's schizophrenic. There's a beautiful person in there." I saw Belle in consultation and agreed that she was indeed a beautiful person.

Belle reported a happy childhood until age 13 when her parents separated. Her mother went to work outside the home, and Belle took care of herself and her 11-year-old sister. Her two older brothers had moved out, and her mother became attached to Belle, who felt responsible for everybody's well-being. At age 15 she became overwhelmed, quit school, and suffered from auditory and visual hallucinations. She saw death, heard the devil talking to her, and felt that she was crazy. At age 17 her father was killed suddenly in an accident, and Belle began taking overdoses of aspirin and other over-the-counter drugs.

Belle went to a clinic, began psychotherapy and, after several weeks, revealed her visual hallucinations. The therapist became alarmed and referred her to a psychiatrist who prescribed anti-psychotic medication, which made Belle tense and clouded her thinking. She became frightened because she felt that she was losing her mind. Responding to her anxiety, the psychiatrist increased the dosage of her medication. Belle began to feel that she was no longer in control of her mind, became overwhelmed, cut herself, and was hospitalized.

After discharge from the hospital, the cycle was repeated. Over a one-year period, Belle had five or six hospitalizations. After each discharge, she cut or burned herself and had to be rehospitalized. After talking to Belle and her mother, I agreed to try therapy if Belle could come five times a week. I thought this frequency would give me a fighting chance to remain engaged with her and to deal with the anticipated stormy disruptions.

Belle and I worked together for five months. The therapy progressed in two phases. In the first phase (about a month), Belle punctually kept her appointments. We became acquainted and she felt understood enough to feel safe and tell me about her past. In the second session she reported a dream where her sister had a baby and put it under the hood of a car "where the motor goes." The car was being chased and then it stopped with smoke pouring out. Belle opened the hood and found the baby dead, burned up. In the analysis of the dream, Belle revealed her feelings of responsibility for taking care of everybody in her family. She was their motor—that was her function. Her mother had never learned to drive, and Belle drove her everywhere. Her siblings were troublemakers, but Belle was good. She never lost her temper or fought with her mother.

In the second phase of therapy Belle had trouble keeping her appointments, and became depressed and discouraged. She thought about death, and worried about losing me, especially if she had to go back into the hospital. I interpreted her fear as a belief that she would be hurting me if she went back into the hospital. That led to new information about Belle's mother's fear of losing her. The mother said that she would die if anything happened to Belle. When Belle had moved out to live with a relative, her mother begged her to come back.

During this phase of the therapy a new dimension of the transference emerged, and our relationship became stormy. After leaving my office, Belle would often drive aimlessly for hours. She would end up in a parking lot where she cut her arms. Twice she admitted herself to the psychiatric unit of a general hospital. I visited her there and, taking an intersubjective stance, I explored what had happened between us in the sessions immediately before the cutting. Like Dorsey, I wanted to get inside her experience.

It was difficult for her to express her disappointment in me and her discouragement with the therapy. She felt cut off and estranged from me, but it had not occurred to her to tell me that. She had not even been aware of those feelings until I used the words *disappointment* and *discouragement*. She had experienced a disruption in our relationship and reacted with feelings of fragmentation. Cutting herself served as an organizing function that helped her to overcome feelings of deadness and chaos and helped her regain a sense of reality and integration.

The intersubjective perspective maintains that investigating the analyst's contribution to the patient's experience of disruption is essential. "The analysis of those innumerable and inevitable experiences of frustration and disappointment in which the patient perceives the analyst as failing in respect to a particular archaic wish or need is an indispensable part of the treatment," is the opinion of Brandchaft and Stolorow (1984a, p. 110).

Belle needed help to develop a vocabulary for her feelings. Words such as *tension*, *fragmentation*, *deadness*, and *emptiness* had a powerful integrating effect when she could connect them with what she had thought of only as "being out of control" or "crazy." She learned later in the therapy that calling someone on the telephone could also help her feel reintegrated.

In the countertransference, I felt anxious, helpless, and guilty each time Belle came in cut and scarred. I felt frustrated and overwhelmed as she repeatedly felt disruptions in our relationship, to which she reacted with self-mutilating behavior. Through my persistent focus on the disruptions in our alliance, she was gradually able to talk about these disruptions, and we were eventually able to get back on track before she cut herself. Support from colleagues helped me through this trying period.

Gradually, Belle felt more integrated, and she began to talk about her sense of pain and guilt over losing her father. She mourned his death, and the hallucinations stopped. She then made plans to move out of her mother's house, at which point her mother abruptly stopped the therapy, announcing that they had run out of money. Belle reacted with renewed determination to move out and not to depend on her mother's money. She felt stronger internally, and she no longer believed that becoming more independent and self-sufficient would destroy her mother.

DISCUSSION

Belle could maintain a sense of integration as long as she felt allied with a strong figure, a concept originally described by Brandchaft and Stolorow (1984b). Her episodes of disintegration were secondary to feelings of disruption in these alliances.

Her previous therapists treated her as though these episodes of disintegration were manifestations of psychopathology arising solely within her. Belle had thus experienced these therapists as telling her what was wrong with her and as prescribing treatments, such as interpretations or medications, to fix her. When she cut herself, the therapists told her that she was getting worse and needed more help. The idea that the cutting was Belle's attempt to help herself, to reintegrate herself, was not perceived, and Belle's strivings for growth and self-help were not recognized.

When Belle would leave my office and cut herself, I assumed that, whatever else was going on within her, there was also a disruption in our alliance that must be looked at first. This disruption was a reaction to her perception of some failure on my part. I wanted to understand my contribution to that perception. If I had yawned, or shifted in my chair or was distracted and looked out the window, Belle assumed that I had lost interest in her. She felt hurt and guilty, yet she was unable to recognize and verbalize those feelings. She merely felt a vague sense of fragmentation, a sensation of being adrift and out of control. She felt disconnected from me, and I no longer existed as a part of her inner world. Her main preoccupation was to counter the feelings of disorganization and internal chaos. Because she needed to re-establish a sense of groundedness, she cut herself. Feeling the pain and seeing the blood provided the stimulation necessary to break through the chaos and give her a focus around which she could reorganize and reintegrate herself.

When I focused our attention on the events immediately before the cutting, and not on the cutting behavior itself, we could identify the experience of a disruption between us. The cutting behavior was then interpreted as a reaction to feelings of disorganization and as an attempt at reintegration. This understanding helped her to reintegrate, and she could then make sense out of what had previously been chaos. Instead of feeling that there was something bad, evil, and destructive in her, she began to experience a sense of validation for her efforts to help herself. Her self-image improved and her self-esteem rose.

When Belle could identify and verbalize such affect states as disappointment, frustration, and discouragement, her sense of integration was re-established. Her mood would brighten and she spontaneously thought that she had distorted my motives or had overreacted. She also recalled new memories of early traumatic experiences that could be integrated into a new sense of a cohesive and deserving self. She no longer felt guilty that she might have a better life than her mother, but came to understand that she had a right to meet her own needs. As Belle became more independent and self-sufficient, her mother finally learned how to become more self-sufficient—she learned how to drive.

Sometimes the line between trusting and worrying about a patient becomes very fine. Trusting patients may help them learn to trust themselves, or it may leave them feeling alone and unprotected. Worrying about patients may come across as intrusive and infantilizing, or it may be reassuring.

Students feel confused, and want to know when to stay with a patient's experience to provide an understanding presence and when to step outside of a patient's experience to confront, for purposes of comparison or examination, with another point of view. Students also want to know how to confront in a spirit of inquiry without being authoritative.

7

Technical
Guidelines

*The true teacher defends his pupils against his own personal
influence. He inspires self-distrust. He guides their eyes
from himself to the spirit that quickens him. He will have
no disciple.*

A. Bronson Alcott

My first analytic supervisor told me to start an analysis by
instructing patients to say what comes to mind, then wait and
make interpretations. My second supervisor said I should first
establish rapport; I should build trust and confidence. The first
supervisor assumed that one would establish rapport, but many
times when I thought I had established rapport, the patient did
not feel connected. I learned not to take the development of
rapport and emotional connection for granted.

Developing rapport with patients is an intuitive process.
Schafer (1974) states: "A real therapeutic relationship is hard
to obtain and is arrived at in unanticipated ways. . . . The con-
duct of therapy . . . is always a matter of weighing one thing
against another and making complex, not altogether certain,
choices" (p. 510).

Maintaining an understanding connection is tricky, like roller
skating in the Himalayas. Each patient will require a variety
of techniques. Sometimes being understanding is what helps,

sometimes repeated repairs of countless disruptions are necessary, and sometimes nothing helps except patience and endurance. The guidelines I suggest for navigating the analytic shoals
are to begin with a careful assessment, and then trust your intuition. At the same time, carefully monitor changes in the
patient's outside life and his or her immediate responses to what
you do, and what you do not do.

ASSESSMENT

The ability to develop rapport is a part of the diagnostic assessment, and the ability to develop a therapeutic relationship is
an indication of suitability for psychoanalysis. I have seen patients who were chaotic, disorganized, and barely functional, yet
something within them touched me; I felt a point of connection.
These patients have done well in analysis. I have seen others
who were well organized and highly functional, yet I could find
no point of connection, and these patients have not done well
in analysis with me. A therapeutic relationship requires rapport plus a relationship where patient and analyst can engage
in a mutual, exploratory adventure. Patients experience some
analysts as easier to work with than others, and analysts find
some patients easier to work with than others. Some patient–
analyst combinations will not be workable. Analysts cannot
determine a patient's suitability for analysis with other analysts—only with themselves. Some patients will express a pref-
erence for working with a woman or a man, and I tell them to
pay serious attention to their intuition. Usually, after two or
three assessment interviews, both patient and analyst will have
a good idea if they are comfortable with each other and can work
together.

An example is Carl, who was good at starting both businesses
and relationships, but was not good at holding onto either. Several successful business ventures ended tragically when his
partners eased him out and took over. Two marriages suffered
similar fates when spouses divorced him, leaving him with few

assets. His present marriage caused him pain and frustration because his wife needed large amounts of money to finance her grown daughter's education. "I don't know how to say no to her," he complained.

For twenty years he turned repeatedly to his best friend from college, a therapist in another community, for support. His friend always had advice and encouragement, but now his friend was frustrated and impatient. "For God's sake," he said, "why don't you see a therapist and get help. You have got to learn to stand up for yourself!" After making inquiries, the friend gave Carl some names, including mine. Carl came to see me, told me his story, and pleaded, "Can you help me?"

"You know what to do," I said, "but something blocks you from doing what you know you need to do to take care of yourself." Carl was pleased, and said, "Yes, if only I could find the courage to say 'No' to others, to not give away everything I have." I told him I would set up some appointments to meet and see what we could understand about this block.

At our next meeting, Carl told me about early experiences of pain and deprivation, about pressures to perform and to take care of his parents, often at his expense. He did not feel he had a right to take care of himself, or that he deserved to have anyone take care of him, beliefs not available to his conscious awareness. When I clarified these beliefs and reflected them back to him, he was impressed. He had not realized they were operating within him in such an automatic way. I was impressed at how insightful he was becoming. Several more sessions were equally powerful. He became aware of how helpless and devoid of inner resources he felt, and surprised that he might have resources within that he could rely on. He also became aware of how irrational was his belief that he was responsible for everyone else and that he had no right to have needs of his own.

Then, in the fourth session, he said to me, "Do you have any answers for me?" I was taken aback, and told him I was puzzled, that I had not thought I would be finding answers for him but that together we would try to understand what blocked him. "If

I have a pain and go to a doctor," he said, "he tells me what's wrong and how to fix it. Aren't you going to tell me what to do? How much longer will it take before you can tell me?" I told him I was surprised, and that I thought what we were talking about was helping him. "Aren't you finding these sessions helpful?" I asked. "No," he answered, "all I get from you are echoes. I want answers, solutions. How do I become able to stand up for myself? How can I learn to say 'No' to my wife?" All of his insight about feeling helpless, about needing to rely on others for advice, and about not trusting that he had resources of his own that could be developed, had vanished. I said, "I thought what we were doing was helping you. This is how I work. If you're not finding it helpful, perhaps you would like to consult another therapist."

He did not want to see another therapist. "I appreciate your honesty," he said. I was disappointed the therapy had not worked, but to my surprise, Carl looked relieved. I realized he came to see me to please the friend who sent him and not because it was what he wanted to do. I revised my assessment: Carl was too compliant to say no to his friend's referral. He wanted to complain and have his friend listen, understand, and not try to fix him or tell him what to do. Although Carl and I had rapport, a treatment alliance was never established.

Doing psychoanalysis has been compared to playing chess. The opening and closing moves are well defined, but the middle game is subject to much variation. Initially, the analyst tunes in to the patient's feelings and tries to understand the patient's experiences. Being patient and understanding goes a long way, but sooner or later, what works initially does not continue to work (Trop and Stolorow 1991). Patients who are initially comfortable with the analyst's passivity and understanding may enter a phase where they become uncomfortable, frustrated, and impatient with the analyst. Or patients who feel reassured and supported by the analyst's activity may enter a phase where the analyst's activity begins to stir up fears of being controlled and invaded.

Students want to know how to decide which way to be. Are there rules to follow? Do you just trust to intuition? Once I have completed the assessment, the patient and I have a mutually agreed upon objective and the analytic process is underway, I rely on these three principles: my personal feeling of authenticity, my assessment of the patient's outside life, and my observation of the patient's immediate response to my intervention.

THE ANALYST'S AUTHENTICITY

Fosshage (1994) defines the analyst's authenticity as a non-defensive presence: "For example, on those occasions when a patient needs a more direct and self-revealing response . . . the analyst's authentic interaction enables the analyst to be more comfortably related to the patient and vice versa" (p. 274). I would expand this definition to include trusting one's intuition, not only about whether to be self-revealing, but also whether to stay with the patient's experience or to confront.

Becoming a psychoanalyst is a developmental process that takes time. Students know more than they realize, but need help in learning to trust themselves, to trust their patients, and to trust the analytic process. If the analyst follows an intuitive hunch and is wrong, it can be a learning experience for analyst and patient. If, however, the analyst goes against intuition and follows a supervisor or theory, a mistake can lead to a disruption, if not to chaos. Chaos can result when the analyst loses confidence, the patient senses it, and they both get scared.

Henry Lihn supervised my analysis of a control case when I was a student at the Los Angeles Psychoanalytic Institute. Lihn always had something new for me to try. When I hesitated in trying his innovative suggestions, he gently encouraged me to try them and see for myself. His ideas worked, and I learned much, but then he made a suggestion that did not fit with my style, and I became uncomfortable, not just hesitant. He continued encouraging me, and I began to feel nagged. Analytic momentum with my patient ceased and the analysis came to a standstill. The analysis was no longer fun. I hated my patient and dreaded our meetings.

During one of these frustrating sessions, my mind wandered. I sat back in my chair staring blankly at the wall opposite me. Suddenly, I had a reverie. At the top of the wall, just below the ceiling, I saw a large glass window, a projection booth. Sitting behind the glass plate, staring down at me, I saw Lihn scrutinizing me.

That was the last straw! I realized I had to enter a confrontive mode with Lihn, and at the next supervisory hour I said to him, "I value your comments, and I want you to feel free to suggest whatever you think I should do, but I must feel free to accept or reject your advice. I am the analyst." Lihn smiled and said gently, "Of course. I didn't realize you were feeling pressured by me. The analysis is going well, and you're doing a fine job. Please feel free to ignore any of my comments that aren't helpful." The analysis resumed its momentum and proceeded to a successful conclusion.

I had fallen into a bind: either I trusted my inclinations or I complied with my supervisor. I began to doubt myself, I lost my authenticity, and I got into trouble. Also, feeling emotionally disconnected from my supervisor, I felt vulnerable with my patient, lost the emotional connection with him, and felt incompetent. Trusting my supervisor, I confronted him and we re-established the supervisory connection. I regained my sense of authenticity and analytic competence.

PATIENTS' OUTSIDE LIFE

Patients enter analysis with some aspect of their personal or professional life in disarray, complaining of problems at home or at work. After a period of therapy, patients' outside lives settle down; relationships improve, and professional work becomes productive. Problems now move into the analytic relationship with tension and frustration in the transference. If the turmoil remains in the transference, treatment is likely on course. If, however, problems re-emerge in patients' outside lives, something in the analysis may be awry. The analyst needs to consider changing tack and perhaps should seek a supervisory consultation.

Bennett, the patient in Chapter 4 who complained that I never said good morning, is an example. Although I knew I said good morning, he claimed otherwise. I stayed with his experience and learned that he was reacting to a certain sleepiness, a lack of spark or enthusiasm, in me. He translated my appearance into a meaning that I had no interest in him. When I understood the impact of my sleepy appearance on him, he stopped complaining that I did not say good morning, progress resumed, and he started criticizing me for other shortcomings. As the negative transference developed, his outside life continued to improve. He now criticized me for emotional aloofness, and protested that I made it difficult for him to feel connected with me. I stayed with his experience and appreciated how hard it was for him to have a cold, impersonal analyst.

His ability to criticize me reflected a new sense of strength and confidence, and indicated that the analysis was on course. But then something changed. He started getting into trouble at work and I felt concerned. Something was mobilized in the transference that I was missing, and I realized that just staying connected with his experience, what I thought was being empathic, was a lack of understanding. I had to pay attention to my concern, to shift gears, and confront him about his behavior. When I finally confronted him, the transference became clear and the analytic momentum resumed.

Another example is Mary, a 26-year-old business woman who entered analysis because of profound depression and hopelessness. Her social life was empty, and she barely functioned at work. After six months of analysis, much of her depression had lifted, and she was again productive at work. Our sessions now became stormy, and I could do nothing right. My interventions caused her pain and humiliation. The analytic work centered on her complaints about me and her feelings of despair in the therapy.

After one year she developed financial problems, and we reduced the sessions from four times a week to twice a week. I soon became aware, however, that her complaints about me had stopped, and she now looked forward to our sessions. I also realized that her depression had recurred and her work productivity was once more impaired. Her feeling of connectedness with me was disrupted, and the analytic process came to a halt. We then worked out a financial plan that allowed us to resume meeting four times a week, and her depression lifted. Her work productivity resumed, and she once more complained bitterly about my treatment of her. Although the sessions were now stormy, I could relax knowing that the analytic process had resumed.

Her despair and hopelessness were feelings from an early age when she was being sexually molested, and she had learned to shut them off from awareness. To be aware of despair, pain, and loneliness was dangerous. It made her mother anxious, and she quickly learned that she would get along better with her mother if she claimed she felt well. She could remember the painful experiences as having occurred, but not their emotional significance, which was minimized. Now she had the opportunity to get in touch with and to begin processing those painful affects.

There can be many reasons for patients developing problems in their outside lives, but if things were going better and a setback occurs in the patient's life, the analyst's initial consideration should be to investigate the therapeutic relationship.

OBSERVATION OF PATIENT'S IMMEDIATE RESPONSE

The findings of empiric research from outside self psychology can help analysts in judging when to stay with a patient's experience and when to be confrontational. The work of Weiss and Sampson (1986) has shown that careful monitoring of a patient's immediate responses to the analyst's interventions provides important cues and can relieve the analyst of much pressure.

Weiss, a San Francisco psychoanalyst, carefully studied detailed process notes from analytic sessions. He looked for patterns and, as a result, developed a theory that patients come to analysis unconsciously knowing what they need to get better. His theory also held that a patient's difficulties result from unconscious pathogenic beliefs of danger, which are dangers that arise if certain developmental goals should be pursued. These grim beliefs are irrational in the present, and are based on early relational experiences. An example of a pathogenic belief is: "If I become more independent and self-sufficient, I will be hurting my mother." Patients will try to use their analysts, Weiss says, in ways that will help them to control and master these beliefs. If, in the course of this new relationship, these beliefs are disconfirmed, the patient becomes free to develop new strategies for achieving developmental goals.

Weiss believes that each patient has an unconscious plan to get better, a plan that of necessity subjects the analyst to tests, which when passed will disconfirm the pathogenic beliefs. In Weiss's theory, when a pathogenic belief is disconfirmed, the patient improves; when the analyst fails a test, a pathogenic belief is confirmed and the patient gets worse.

Weiss's research shows that direct observation of a patient's immediate response to the analyst's intervention can indicate if the intervention was pro-plan or anti-plan. If the patient responds in a bold, direct, and insightful manner, the analyst is on target. If, however, the patient responds in a diffuse, anxious, and resistant manner, then the analyst is off track.

The challenge for the psychoanalyst is to stay connected to the patient in a way that furthers the psychoanalytic process. A contribution of self psychology and of intersubjectivity theory is that the patient's response to what we do—and to what we do not do—becomes the focus of investigation. Empathic inquiry allows us to assess what happens when we stay with the patient's experience and what happens when we confront the patient with *our* experience. The focus is not on whether we stay with a patient's experience or confront a patient; it is on the impact of each of these behaviors. Using intuition, assessing the patient's outside life, and watching the patient's immediate response helps us to understand this impact and to stay connected.

8

Control
Mastery Theory

Order and simplification are the first steps toward the mastery of a subject—the actual enemy is the unknown.
                                                                Thomas Mann

In 1986, Weiss, Sampson, and the Mount Zion Psychotherapy Research Group (1986) published *The Psychoanalytic Process: Theory, Clinical Observation and Empirical Research*, the culmination of fourteen years of empiric research. Following the book's publication, colleagues in San Francisco invited me to a workshop to study these ideas and the research. Since that time, in a mutual collaboration, I have taught my colleagues about self psychology while immersing myself in the study of their research. Control Mastery theory is slowly finding its way into the psychoanalytic literature (Eagle 1993; Silverman 1989).

An audio recording and some hours of process notes of a completed analysis, the case of Mrs. C., were made available to the research group. The treating analyst knew nothing about Weiss or his theory, and had recorded the analysis for his personal research. Working from a classical model, he considered the terminated analysis a success. The research group looked at these materials and formulated the patient's unconscious plan and pathogenic beliefs.

PLAN FORMULATION

One group of research workers, reading transcripts of the opening hours, formulated the patient's "plan." Plan formulations have four parts: the patient's goals are inferred, obstructions or pathogenic beliefs are inferred, tests that the therapist will be subjected to are predicted, and insights that will help the patient are predicted (Curtis et al. 1988).[1]

After formulating the patient's plan, the researchers looked at samples of the analyst's interventions excerpted from transcripts of the recordings. Without knowing the patient's responses, the workers rated each intervention on a scale from pro-plan to anti-plan.

A second group of research workers, knowing nothing about the plan formulated or the analyst's interventions, looked only at transcripts of the patient's responses, rating them on a scale from "bold, strong, and insightful" to "diffuse, anxious, and resistant." The results showed a statistically significant correlation between interventions rated as pro-plan with patient responses that were rated as bold, strong, and insightful, and anti-plan interventions correlated with diffuse, anxious, and resistant responses.

ASSESSING RESPONSES

The research shows that direct observation of a patient's immediate response can determine whether the analyst's intervention is pro-plan or anti-plan. For example, when the analyst's behavior or intervention disconfirms the pathogenic belief, a pro-plan response, the patient's immediate response is bolder,

---

1. Control Mastery therapists infer a patient's plan in the first few hours and use this formulation to guide their interpretations. I prefer a "wait and see" mode of investigation. Patients have good reasons for their behavior, and by monitoring their responses to my interventions, I believe their plan will become clear in time.

stronger and more insightful. When the analyst confirms the pathogenic belief, an anti-plan response, the patient's immediate response is more diffuse, anxious, and resistant.

What if the patient is complaining about a lack of progress in the therapy? Careful attention to the patient's affect and state of integration, not just his or her words, can determine if this is progress or a setback. If the patient is complaining in a more anxious and fragmented way, the analyst is anti-plan, and a change is indicated. If the patient, however, was previously feeling chaotic and disorganized and is now complaining in a bolder, stronger, more integrated fashion, then the analyst is pro-plan. Thinking "This is just a test" will help the analyst stay calm (Weiss 1993).

Patients, on the other hand, may agree with the analyst because the interpretation fits for them, or they may agree out of a sense of compliance. When my patients comply, the life goes out of them; they appear passive and I feel disconnected from them. Their diffuseness and lack of vitality indicate that I have been anti-plan. When the patient's agreement with me is bold, strong, and vital, it indicates that I have been pro-plan.

PATIENTS' TESTS

Weiss states that patients unconsciously test their therapists to determine if conditions are safe. When therapists pass such tests, patients feel safe. Unconscious material then spontaneously emerges into conscious awareness (Gassner et al. 1982). No special interpretation or activity by the analyst is necessary.

> The patient tests the therapist from the beginning to the end of treatment. He is vitally interested in finding out how the therapist will react to his plans. Will the therapist oppose his goals, or will he be sympathetic to them and encourage him to pursue them? The therapist's ability to recognize the patient's tests and pass them is central to

therapy. The success or failure of a therapy may depend
on this. [Weiss 1993, p. 92]

This way of thinking helped me with Joan, a patient who, for
the first six months of her analysis, was scrupulously punctual.
Then she started coming late, often ten or twenty minutes late,
apologizing profusely each time. Thinking initially that this was
a resistance, I wondered aloud if the chronic lateness was an
expression of underlying anger toward me. She felt hurt and
criticized by this formulation, and gradually became depressed
and discouraged. Our treatment alliance was disrupted and an
impasse developed.

I then learned about pathogenic beliefs and realized that her
belief was that if she acted independently, she would hurt me. She
was testing me, and I was giving her the message that coming
late was hurting me. I was failing the test, and she was anxious.
Now I understood that she was trying to develop a sense of her
own individuality, to give up being the compliant, good little girl.
My attitude changed, I stopped taking her lateness personally,
and I passed her test. Her mood improved, her sense of confidence
returned, and the treatment alliance was re-established.

I understood, and explained to her, that she came late because
she was busy taking care of other business. She was, for the first
time, doing things for herself, not just for everyone else (including me). Her pathogenic belief was that doing something for
herself was selfish and hurt others, and she did not have a right
to do something just for herself. Her unconscious test was to
take care of herself and see if that hurt me.

When I interpreted the lateness as anger directed at me, I
failed the test and confirmed her belief that taking care of herself hurt me. When I understood that she was feeling the freedom to decide how to run her life, to decide whether to stay at
her office and finish her work or to come to her appointment, I
passed the test and her pathogenic belief was disconfirmed.

Weiss describes two types of tests: transferring tests and passive into active tests. In a transferring test, the patient will

anticipate a traumatic response from the analyst similar to one received from earlier caregivers. This test is easily passed by sensitive analysts who respond in a validating or acknowledging way when the patient is expecting to be criticized or discounted. Taking a patient seriously may disconfirm a pathogenic belief that the patient's complaints will injure the analyst. It may also meet developmental needs for acknowledgment in the selfobject dimension of the transference (Stolorow and Lachmann 1980).

Passive into active tests occur when a patient, in an identification with a traumatizing parent, subjects the analyst to abuses similar to those experienced in childhood. For instance, a patient subjected to criticism and humiliation in growing up, in an attempt at control and mastery, will unconsciously, and often subtly, provoke and belittle the analyst, while carefully monitoring the analyst's responses. If the analyst acts hurt or becomes defensive, the patient's belief will be confirmed. The patient will continue to believe that he or she is supposed to organize around meeting the analyst's needs, and will continue to feel vulnerable and responsible. If, however, the analyst survives the attack, can take care of himself or herself and not blame the patient, the pathogenic belief will be disconfirmed. Seeing the analyst as strong and not vulnerable, the patient will then identify with the analyst's strength in the process of mastering the underlying feeling of vulnerability.[2]

Passive into active tests are more stressful for therapists than are transferring tests:

> When the patient transfers, he endows the therapist with the authority of a parent, so the therapist tends to feel

---

2. Weiss believes that analysts may do the right thing for the wrong reasons. After reviewing the analyst's process notes in the case of Mrs. C., Weiss believes that the patient made progress despite the fact that many of the analyst's interpretations were out of tune with what the patient was working on. Something about the analyst's personality and manner passed some important tests (Personal Communication 1987).

relatively safe. However, when he turns passive into active, the patient assumes the role of the traumatizing parent, and the therapist may feel considerable strain. [Weiss 1993, p. 105]

When I feel abused by patients—belittled, discounted, taken for granted—if I can consider that I am now the target of a passive into active test, I often find myself saying something like, "I understand more clearly what you've been saying about feeling abused in growing up." My countertransference feelings are related to subtle, unconscious communications. Patients, being sensitive and intuitive, can automatically and unconsciously sense my areas of vulnerability, and will use this knowledge to test me.

For example, if I feel a need to be helpful, my patient may sense it and start feeling helpless. If I react by trying harder to be helpful, to "fix" the problems, my patient may become anxious. If, instead, I try to understand the helpless feelings and to explore the underlying vulnerability, my patient may feel stronger.

My trying to be more helpful derived in part from internal feelings of pressure to perform and to feel effective. When my patient complained of helplessness and anxiety, I felt guilty; I felt ineffective as a therapist, and believed I had not done my job. Patients who grow up feeling responsible for, and pressured to fix their anxious parents will feel irrational guilt and responsibility for the anxiety of others. When they sense a similar guilt and responsibility in me, they will automatically act helpless and stir me up. When I react with guilt and try harder to help, it confirms their pathogenic belief. If I believe that I am responsible for them, they believe that they are responsible for their parents, and they become anxious. When I can stay calm and investigative, however, it reassures patients that, since I do not feel I have to fix them, maybe they do not have to feel so pressured to fix others.

Weiss believes that pathogenic beliefs may be directly modified through experience and insight. Because pathogenic beliefs are frightening and debilitating, patients are unconsciously motivated to change them and highly active in their efforts to seek out experiences that will disprove them.

UNCONSCIOUS GUILT

In discussing pathogenic beliefs, Weiss elaborates on the concept of guilt. He gives unconscious guilt more central importance than does self psychology, and he links it to unconscious pathogenic beliefs. His contribution has been summarized by Bush (1989):

> Irrational unconscious guilt stems from distorted unconscious beliefs about having done something bad in the fundamental sense of doing something hurtful or being disloyal to another person toward whom one feels a special sense of attachment or responsibility, such as a parent, sibling, or child. . . . [This model of guilt] emphasizes the primacy of the individual's fear of hurting others as the deepest unconscious layer of the experience of guilt. [p. 98]

Weiss describes two types of guilt: separation guilt and survivor guilt. Based on early traumatic experiences and not on unconscious drives, children can develop beliefs that separation or self-individuation will hurt a parent (separation guilt), or that whatever they get for themselves will be at someone else's expense (survivor guilt). Self psychologists have contributed much to our understanding of separation fears and the extent to which children will go to protect themselves against a loss of vital connections with caregivers (Kohut 1984, Stolorow et al. 1987). Weiss adds another dimension with his belief that children also have conflicts because of love and feelings of loyalty toward caregivers. The child may be more afraid of hurting a parent than of losing a parent.

I believe the two conflicts, fear of loss and fear of being bad or disloyal, have a figure-ground relationship to each other. Sometimes the fear of loss will be more in the foreground than the fear of being disloyal. In one example, a patient was struggling to express her criticism of me. I interpreted that she was afraid of losing me if she told me her complaints. "I'm not afraid of losing you!" she said, "I know you will hang in there with me, but I don't want you to see me as bad." She then told me that complaints to her mother resulted in mother accusing her of being "evil." Her mother saw the "devil" inside her. At another time in the analysis, she was reluctant to tell me her critical feelings for fear that I would be hurt and withdraw from her. This time she was not worried I would think she was bad, but she feared losing the connection with me.

The challenge for the psychoanalytic therapist is to stay connected with the patient and to aid in the orderly unfolding of material that is the psychoanalytic process. If our patients do not feel connected with us, our interpretations—no matter how brilliant—will have no effect.

9

Connecting
with Despair

It is a time when one's spirit is subdued and sad, one knows not why; when the past seems a storm-swept desolation, life a vanity and a burden, and the future but a way to death.
                                                                    Mark Twain

Angel, a 19-year-old college student, worried me. An attractive, willowy girl, she first consulted me after being found by a roommate asleep in the back seat of her car in a closed garage with the motor running. Angel's unsuccessful attempt on her life did not stem from depression, but from feeling that something was wrong with her, that she just did not belong in this world. "Something is wrong with my thinking," she said. "I need help."

In this challenging case I used concepts from Control Mastery theory and from self psychology to help me stay connected with her despair. Separation guilt, a central concept of Control Mastery theory, was a major factor blocking Angel in her self-individuation. A lack of affect integration, a central concept of self psychology, handicapped her ability to understand her emotional needs. Angel needed me to tune in and give voice to her emotional states, a selfobject function, and she unconsciously needed to subject me to tests that would help resolve her separation guilt.

COURSE OF THERAPY

Intensive work with young people with developmental arrests often can achieve much progress in a short time, and Angel's analysis lasted just five months. We made a good connection and she felt understood in our first session, so we decided to meet five times a week. However, our connection vanished over the first weekend break and our meetings the following week left me feeling frustrated and anxious. She would talk about anything that I wanted. I wanted to know about her and what she wanted, but she expressed no desires of her own. I could not find the key to reconnecting, and my anxiety increased because I believed she could commit suicide at any time and without warning.

After two weeks of feeling disconnected, I concluded that she was protecting herself because she felt vulnerable and afraid to trust me. I tried sharing my feelings of frustration and disconnection with her, and she relaxed. My reaching out to her by sharing my feelings disconfirmed her belief that she had to do all the work and be alone. I asked whether disconnection from family and friends left her feeling sad, lonely and in pain. Her reaction to my saying words like "sad" or "lonely" or "pain" was, "It's not good to feel that way. You don't want me to feel that way." These feelings, which had seemed dangerous, had been walled off, but now she could experience and integrate them.

She said she realized that she had been in a rut and was living a constricted existence. She thought it would be a long road out of that self-imposed prison, and told me she felt paralyzed with self-consciousness, often holding her breath when around other people. These behaviors, which had been automatic, were now becoming conscious.

I found myself subjected to a series of self-assertion tests as she began to express her individuality. For example, she was floundering during one session and complained that I did not help her to get started. "You could at least say hello when I come in," she said, and then apologized for being rude. What she experienced as rudeness I experienced as awkward self-assertiveness. I inferred that she wanted to get over feeling that she hurt people by asserting herself, and asked if she apologized because she felt she was hurting me when she asserted herself. Her response was bold and insightful: "Taking care of myself is being mean—it makes me feel guilty." My interpretation helped her disconfirm her belief that asserting herself hurt others.

She then looked for my permission to take off her shoes, to sit with her feet tucked under, and to bring a soft drink to session. I interpreted these requests as her feeling under pressure to figure out what I expected so that she could comply. Her response was to realize the pressures she felt from family and friends to do things "right," and her feeling of shame if she did not comply. She feared that she would hurt me, as she believed she hurt her mother, if she took care of herself. She then realized that she felt, automatically and unconsciously, that it was her duty to take care of others, even at her expense. Something must be wrong with her, she had reasoned, because she could never do enough, and people were always needing more from her. She had reached a point where she could not give any more, and believed that she did not belong in this world. Feeling desperate for relief, she decided to kill herself.

As I systematically interpreted her separation guilt in the transference, her feeling, for example, that disagreements would hurt me, she became more sure of herself. She realized that she had ambitions and goals, and she had a right to pursue them. She became less compliant, reached out more to her friends, and, to her surprise, people responded positively. Saying "No" to one of her friends was a new experience. "It was like getting a piece of gunk off of me!" she said.

Feeling stronger now led to further testing, and she barraged me with personal questions about where I live, how old I am, and whether I have children. Appreciating these questions as aspects of her newfound courage in reaching out, and not as intrusions, I answered each question without hesitation. She became anxious after telling me that she did not like one of my paintings. She feared that expressing her own ideas and opinions would hurt me if they did not agree with my way of thinking.

Becoming more self-reflective, she realized how isolated she had become from her friends. She said that everyone expected her to listen to their problems, but no one reached out to her. "People look to me to be a den mother," she said. "At my last birthday party I could have been dead or not there. It wouldn't have mattered."

When she described another irritating situation I pointed out that she sounded apologetic for complaining. She recalled how, when growing up, complaining was not nice and was not allowed. She had gotten the message that complaints, or any expressions of painful feelings, would hurt other people. After the first month of therapy, when her friends asked what happened to her, she could talk about her suicide attempt. Becoming more aware of her feelings, she felt more in control and less afraid. Hope had returned.

Life now excited her, and after three months of therapy, she wanted to reduce the sessions to three times a week. She explained that our appointments were a "touchstone" for her, a place where she could organize and focus, but she wanted time to think about things before coming in. Staying connected with me was no longer a problem; she could pick up where she left off, even after the weekend break. I experienced this as a test to see if I needed her to fulfill my therapeutic ambitions. I understood that she wanted to see what she could do on her own, without talking to me first, an idea I thought worth trying. With her increasing self-confidence, she went on to develop new relationships and to have new experiences of mutuality, intimacy, and aliveness. She then began canceling and missing appointments.

I understood the missed appointments as tests to see if I trusted her to run her own life, or if I needed her to meet my narcissistic needs like her mother did. At one point, however, after not seeing or hearing from her for a week, I became anxious, began to doubt my assessment, and called her. My call came while she was asleep, and she was angry. She said, "I'm not feeling well. Do you want me to come in?" I said that I had not meant to intrude, but wondered if there had been some misunderstanding. She said that there was no misunderstanding, but she failed to keep the next appointment. Later that day she left a message apologizing for being rude by not calling me to cancel the appointment.

At the next appointment, she asked anxiously if I still wanted her as a patient. I said I had called because I felt anxious, and had not meant to pressure her. When I heard that she was not well, I realized that she was taking care of herself and was not off somewhere trying to commit suicide. I did not think she would commit suicide, I added, but I did not know her that well yet. "You can't always be sure," she said sympathetically, and she said she felt guilty for wasting my time. I explained that she was responsible to pay for the time, but the time was hers to use in whatever way she felt was best. She brightened and said, "I felt this was one place where I wouldn't have to worry." I said that our goal was for her to be able to take care of herself without having to worry about taking care of me and everybody else first. When her initial anxiety changed into a confident brightness, I felt reassured that although I failed one test by calling her, I had passed her next test, her fear that I would reject her for not complying, and we re-established our therapeutic connection.

In the following weeks, she came to her appointments intermittently, calling only a few times to cancel. Her insightfulness and assertiveness, however, continued to blossom, and she continued to have meaningful new experiences. Her relationship with her mother also improved, and they developed a strong connection.

I went on vacation, and she did well during my absence. She then asked me about cutting the sessions down to twice a week, explaining that "there is a danger zone, a time when something is not right with your thinking, and there is a reality zone, a time of discovery and of learning new things." She no longer was in danger, she was continuing to learn new things, and she felt certain that her progress would continue. She asked what I thought. I said that I didn't know what was best, but I would encourage her to follow her hunches and see what happened. If things continued to improve, that would be a good sign. If problems arose, we could re-evaluate the decision to cut down. She thought about her unhappy, self-concious high school experiences, and wondered what she might have done had she been feeling as good then as she did now.

She came on time for the next session, but found herself reluctant to come and was puzzled. Coming to the sessions no longer felt the same, and she asked me why I thought she did not want to come. Looking for a precipitant, I asked if anything had come up in our last session that distressed her. When she said no, I said that perhaps the original reason for coming, that something was not right with her thinking, no longer applied. Perhaps it was time to reassess our goals and to review our options.

She asked me about options, and I said that one was to take a break, to have a period of time on her own, and then meet and review her experience. Another option would be to change our focus from current problems and explore underlying issues. Thinking that her query was a resistance, I said that I would encourage her to continue the therapy and explore underlying issues, especially if she hoped to have a family some day and wanted her children to have better experiences. That made sense to her, but she did not want to have children, and, quite boldly, she said she did not want to look at underlying issues. She wanted to take a break, but worried that if she stopped, she could not come back.

I paid close attention to her immediate responses. When I explored the idea of her continuing, she became more diffuse and anxious. When I explored the idea of taking a break, she became bolder and more confident. Taking my cue from her responses, I agreed to terminate and meet in six weeks for a re-evaluation.

She arrived for this follow-up appointment on time and reported continued progress. She said, apologetically, that she did not miss the sessions. I interpreted her fear that feeling independent and self-sufficient would be hurting me. She immediately brightened and reported that she had finally verbalized complaints to her roommate and, as a result, their relationship improved. She also reported that she felt strong enough to finally quit her heavy cigarette smoking. (She had never discussed her smoking habit with me.) Her parents, too, had changed, and were reconsidering their values about life—they were learning from her.

She remembered that she had stopped laughing in junior high school when she started learning to "be a lady." She had worried that people thought she was weird, and she felt that there was something about her that put people off, something unpleasant or unattractive. Now she felt happy, laughed a lot, and was no longer preoccupied with other people's reactions. She was pleased that she no longer felt something was wrong with her, and she wanted to terminate. Four months later I received a Christmas card with a note: "Everything has been great lately. It's exciting to look forward to the new year. Thank you very much for your help. You helped me begin to make enormous changes in my life. I feel better than I've *ever* felt."

DISCUSSION

To summarize her testing: My self-disclosure of feeling frustrated passed a test showing her that I would work with her and not leave her to fend for herself. Her pathogenic belief that she did not have a right to have help, that she had to do everything on her own, was disconfirmed. She then felt safe enough to test me further by asserting her individuality while carefully monitoring my responses. Transferring tests included her anticipating my withdrawing from her, as her mother did, if she did not comply with my expectations. A passive into active test was her withdrawing from me, as Mother did from her, and looking to see if I would become anxious as she did. The time when I became anxious and called her, I failed the test. She came into the next session anxious and compliant, anticipating that I no longer wanted her as a patient. The failed test was not a technical error, but an inadvertent disruption characteristic of any therapy, and an opportunity for further investigation. The word "fail" does not mean the analyst did anything wrong. It refers only to the patient's perception: in self psychology it comes up as "empathic failure" and in Control Mastery theory it comes up as "failed test."

CONCLUSION

I believe that experienced therapists from differing theoretical perspectives intuitively infer their patients' unconscious plans, and unconsciously pass tests that disconfirm their patients' pathogenic beliefs. Such therapists also unconsciously provide selfobject functions for their patients that help overcome developmental blocks.

When treatment goes well, one can trust one's theoretical beliefs, but when treatment bogs down, when impasses develop, one can be helped by looking at contributions from other theoretical points of view. In classical theory, treatment impasses are viewed as "negative therapeutic reactions," as manifestations of forces arising solely from within the patient (Brandchaft 1983). In both self psychology and Control Mastery theories, impasses are seen as the result of something gone awry in the intersubjective field: either analysts are not seeing something from the patient's perspective, or analysts are failing a test. Analysts need to immerse themselves further in the patient's subjective world or to infer more accurately the patient's plan.

Self psychology has contributed much to the literature on patients' struggles with fears of loss and rejection, and the need to maintain vital ties. Sometimes, however, the fear of hurting the loved object is more pertinent than the fear of losing the loved object. Addressing the concepts of separation guilt and survivor guilt is a helpful contribution of Control Mastery theory.

Fundamental to self psychology is an appreciation of the selfobject function of affect attunement in the development of affect integration (Shapiro 1991, Socarides and Stolorow 1984/1985). One aspect of affect integration is the ability to identify and to put into words internal feeling states. The development of speech in the child helps to process painful feelings. A block in the development of affect integration leaves an individual vulnerable to being overwhelmed by tension and to secondary feelings of chaos, fragmentation, or painful paralysis.

Angel's suicide attempt was a desperate try to get relief from such pain, to free herself from an intolerable and relentless feeling of enslavement. I said that she was like the citizens of New Hampshire whose state slogan is "Live Free or Die!"

With some patients, my attempt to be understanding when they want to reduce sessions or terminate leads to anxiety. They feel rejected and unwanted. With Angel, however, understanding her wish to stop resulted in increased boldness and insightfulness.

Angel's abrupt termination raises the question of a "flight into health," but suddenly stopping treatment can also meet developmental needs. Patients may need to have the experience of seeing what they can do for themselves and still feel the therapist's support. They may return for more therapy with the same therapist or with a different therapist, and work on other issues. This is a natural developmental experience and is not a shortcoming of the original therapy (Goldberg and Marcus 1985, Malin 1990). To interpret the stopping only as running away or acting out prevents these patients from feeling pleased with their accomplishment.

There are many ways to understand a therapy. Angel's case shows how the self psychology concept of selfobject functioning and the Control Mastery concept of passing tests to disconfirm pathogenic beliefs complemented each other and helped me keep my bearings and stay connected while working with this challenging patient.

10

The
Psychoanalytic
Process

The moment of truth, the sudden emergence of a new insight, is an act of intuition. Such intuitions give the appearance of miraculous flushes, or short-circuits of reasoning. In fact they may be likened to an immersed chain, of which only the beginning and the end are visible above the surface of consciousness. The diver vanishes at one end of the chain and comes up at the other end, guided by invisible links.

Arthur Koestler

I love figuring out how things work, discovering the invisible, unconscious links that help make sense of my experiences and those of others. To understand the problems of the mind and to treat them is a major challenge, but even more challenging is to explain and make clear how this is accomplished.

Students have a similar problem explaining their work. At one time or another, they need to write case reports, which describe the psychoanalytic process. While students have little difficulty describing the content of an hour in terms of what was said by them and their patients, they become paralyzed when asked to show the orderly unfolding of material that is the psychoanalytic process.

Psychoanalytic process is a term that gets bandied about as though everyone knows what it means, yet there is no consensus for its definition. *Process* refers to a series of actions or changes taking place in a systematic or definite manner. In an analysis, process refers to at least two different phenomena:

- The orderly or systematic unfolding of material, by which is meant the sequence of thoughts, feelings, and meanings of experience that take place during a session.
- The operations that take place, the invisible links, between the time of an experience and the meaning that accrues to that experience. That is, process can refer to the ways that experiences become organized into a schema or diagram, the ways that experiences develop into an organizing principle.

THE ORDERLY UNFOLDING OF MATERIAL

In 1959, Karl Menninger, a pioneer in developing a theory of psychoanalytic technique (Menninger and Holzman 1973), described an orderly sequence of material in a "properly going" analysis where the material flows from the *present* to the *transference* to the *past* and then back to the *present*.

> The patient will usually describe, for example, an aspect of the *reality* situation that he finds unpleasant, and from this go to certain aspects of the *analytic* situation. . . . Under the aegis of . . . the analytic situation his mind reverts to childhood, and he recalls something from that area. . . . From this area he soon turns again to the present . . . and a cycle will have been completed. [pp.154–155]

Menninger goes on to state that a flow of material in the wrong direction, from the present directly to the past without going through the transference, is a manifestation of resistance.

When I first read this description of the psychoanalytic process thirty years ago, it intrigued me. Carefully watching my own analytic work since then has convinced me of its merits. It is schematic, however, and is useful only if not taken too seriously. Many times, for instance, either analyst or patient will go productively from present to past without going through the transference, and many times there will be much productive analytic work with no mention of the transference. We must be careful not to nag our patients if we think they are avoiding the transference.

Nevertheless, Menninger's theory continues to intrigue me, and integrating Menninger's idea with self psychology, particularly with the concept of affect attunement (Socarides and Stolorow 1984/1985, Stolorow et al. 1987), I have developed a view of the psychoanalytic process that helps me organize my thinking. In listening to clinical material, I look for four factors: affect and the emergence of transference, resistance to the emerging transference, interpretation of resistance, and response to interpretation. This view of the psychoanalytic process is a guide, not a formula.

Affect and the Emergence of Transference

The patient begins a session talking about something in the present, which Menninger says is usually something unpleasant. I try to identify more specifically the affect, the patient's emotional experience. It may be a feeling of frustration, disappointment, irritation, helplessness, or vulnerability. Once I sense the affect, I listen for the emergence of transference, for evidence that these feelings might also relate to me, but I do not say anything; I wait to see if there is resistance to the emergence of transference.

Resistance to the Emerging Transference

If the flow of material is orderly, as Menninger describes, then the material will move spontaneously from the present to the transference, and I do not have to make an interpretation. If,

however, the patient becomes stuck in the present or moves
directly to the past without going through the transference, then
I will consider that there may be resistance, the repetitive dimension of the transference (Stolorow et al. 1987), and I will
ask a question or make an interpretation.

Interpretation of Resistance

The repetitive dimension of the transference occurs when a
habitual and problematic manner of organizing the experience
of a relationship is brought to bear on the analytic relationship.
A man may complain that his employer treats him in a conde-
scending or humiliating way, and I will wonder to myself if that
also relates to his experience of me. I do not assume, however,
that it *must* relate to me, and if he moves on to other emotionally laden material, I will stay with his experience. But if he
becomes repetitious, seems stuck in the present, or suddenly
talks about the past, I will suspect resistance to the emergence
of transference. He may be feeling that I treat him in a conde-
scending or humiliating way, but he fears that awareness of this
affect will disrupt our relationship. I will inquire, "When you
assert yourself with your employer, he responds in a condescend-
ing or humiliating way. Is some of that stirred up in here? Do
you sometimes experience me that way?"

If he acknowledges that experience with me, I will inquire
further about the resistance: "Is there something that makes
it hard to share these feelings with me?" If he is struggling, I
will try to identify the affect: "You seem tense in talking about
this. Are you feeling some uneasiness?" I assume that his resistance is in anticipation of a painful or traumatic response from
me. Even Greenson, a classical analyst, says, ". . . the main
motive for resistance and for defense is to avoid pain" (1967,
p. 82).

From an intersubjective perspective, I assume that the pain
being avoided is anticipated as coming from me. The patient
might say, "I don't want to hurt your feelings—then you won't

like me." At that point I will investigate if I have contributed to the experience, and might ask, "Is there something I have said or done to indicate my insensitivity to your complaints?" If the patient says, "No, it has nothing to do with you," then I back off. Although this may be resistance, it may also be that I have made a mistake. If there is resistance, it will become clear in time; I do not need to be pushy.

John was telling me about his difficulty in relaxing, and also describing the continual pressure he felt to perform. While he was talking, I heard a racket outside my window and turned my head briefly to glance outside. A few minutes later I noticed that John was yawning and becoming vague. I couldn't follow what he was talking about, and he looked uncomfortable.

Could this be a resistance to the emergence of transference? Was he reacting to something about me and afraid to recognize it? Tuning in to his affect I asked, "Is something worrying you?" "You looked out the window, and I felt you were bored, that I wasn't being interesting," he replied.

My distraction had a meaning for him of rejection and criticism—he was failing to keep me interested. His withdrawal was automatic, and he had not realized it until I noticed a change. Recognizing and verbalizing his transference feelings, feelings that I was bored by him, he spontaneously remembered how his father would look away. "My father was depressed, and I could never engage him," he said, "I didn't realize he was depressed, I just assumed I wasn't interesting to him." Then with much sadness he said, "I tried over and over to please him, to be admired by him." When the resistance was resolved John spontaneously recalled memories about his father and experienced feelings of sadness.

Response to Interpretation

Once I have made an intervention, I look very carefully at the patient's immediate response. If I have been accurate, there will often be resolution of the resistance and the experiencing of new affect, perhaps in the form of tears or anger, and new material from the past.

An example is Joe, a 37-year-old engineer who entered analysis because, although tired of being alone, he was unable to maintain a relationship. Four years earlier, his wife divorced him after seven years of marriage. He has not had a relationship since.

He began a Monday hour, six months into the analysis, complaining about his lonely weekend. In a bored, discouraged tone, he described hanging around his house, watching TV, going to a movie by himself, and worrying about his diet. (He is trying to lose weight so he will feel more confident and be more attractive to women.) "I feel tired," he said. Experiencing him as distant and withdrawn, I said, "You *seem* tired." That comment engaged him.

Coming more alive, he told me about his weekend craving for pizza. After much struggle, he gave in, had a piece, felt guilty and dissatisfied, and wondered why he even bothered. Trying to attune to his affect, I said, "You seem discouraged." "Yeah," he said, "You'd think I'd learn!" He then withdrew, became distant, and grumbled, "There's got to be something better."

The momentary aliveness now gone, I suspected he was discouraged with me but felt fearful about experiencing and expressing discouragement. Approaching the transference I said, "Are you feeling some discouragement in here with me, some frustration that things should be better by now?" He replied cautiously, "I have learned some things, but I feel impatient, and I want it to be over. I want to live, but I know it doesn't work that way. I'm not disappointed, but I'm not encouraged either. I'm still just as alone."

Trying to reflect his discouragement and strengthen our connection, I suggested, "It is hard to feel hopeful when you still feel so alone." "Especially on this diet," he said more strongly. Then, in a more discouraged tone: "I'm just filling time, just waiting for something to happen." As he became more diffuse, I again tried to connect with his affect and asked, "Are you feeling disappointed?" Still resistant, he said, "No, we're going on. It's interesting. I think about this stuff. There is just no way to apply anything, no plan." He became silent and seemed tense.

I interpreted the resistance: "You seem more tense when talking about your disappointment in here with me." His tension abated, and he said movingly, "How can I tell you? That would mean something is wrong with you, that the analysis isn't working." Now with new vitality, he described his fear that his complaints would hurt me and, in retaliation, I would respond by pushing him away. I echoed his fear: "I would be hurt and would reject you." "That's what *I* do," he said. "At work, if someone complains, I tell them: 'You want my help or not? If not, go somewhere else!'"

Our connection was now re-established, and he went on to tell me that this is what he was used to. In his marriage, any expression of frustration or disappointment led to his wife feeling unloved, and she pulled away from him. "I learned that it's better to keep that stuff to yourself," he said.

Further clarifying his resistance, I said, "What a dilemma. You have to keep your feelings to yourself to keep from hurting me, and to protect yourself from being rejected by me. The price, then, is to be isolated and alone in here." He was moved by this interpretation, and recalled new memories of isolation and loneliness in growing up. An only child, his mother insisted on his being "positive" and "keeping up appearances." Any expression of pain or annoyance caused her to feel hurt, to feel she had failed. His father avoided conflict each evening by turning on the TV and drinking himself into a stupor.

We came to appreciate how, in growing up, he felt responsible for his mother's shame and his father's withdrawal. He learned at an early age to automatically sense uneasiness in others and to take care of them, even at his own expense. Now when he sensed any uneasiness in his current relationships or with me he felt the same responsibility.

This example illustrates the psychoanalytic process: first I tuned in to his affect—his feeling of discouragement and disappointment. Then his disappointment emerged in the transference—he felt disappointed in me. Anxiety about hurting me then led to resistance to the emergence of this transference feeling. Interpretation of the resistance, that he feared I would be hurt and would reject him, led to new memories, to a new feeling of aliveness in himself and to a connectedness with me. This was his response to the interpretation.

Using this way of organizing the flow of material, students find they can succinctly write up a clinical hour, a series of hours, or an entire psychoanalysis. In listening to what their patients say and watching how they say it, students find it helpful to track three components of clinical material:

- *Content*—the subject of a patient's discussion.
- *Affect*—the emotional tone, or lack of emotional tone, associated with the content.
- *Process*—the operations taking place between the time of an experience and the meaning associated with that experience, or the way in which an experience becomes organized into a schema or diagram. (This is the second definition of "process" referred to earlier in this chapter.)

MEANINGS OF EXPERIENCE

Experiences are often associated with unconscious meanings. An experience of disappointment may come to have a meaning of shame and humiliation; an experience of frustration may translate, automatically and without conscious awareness, into a meaning of being unlovable. An experience of success may subtly and unconsciously change into a feeling of being bad or naughty. The investigation of these subtle shifts in affect state helps to illuminate the process, the unconscious organizing principles.

Early in my development I focused mainly on content to the exclusion of affect and process. I was impressed by teachers who found underlying meanings in everything a patient said, did, or dreamed. I thought they had a secret code I needed to learn.

One patient talked about the unstable economic climate and predicted an economic depression. The supervisor confidently said that the patient was really talking about his underlying depression—a depression, in fact, related to an early loss of the breast. There was no inquiry about the emotional feeling tone associated with the patient's discussion of depression.

A way to investigate the emotional feeling tone would be to inquire whether the patient was talking about a pending economic depression in a subdued, withdrawn, or emotionally flattened manner, which would be an indication of an emerging depression, or whether the patient was predicting the future in a bold, confident manner, which would be an expression of emerging new confidence and competence. I remember Ralph Greenson telling us in an analytic seminar to look at affect before content. That good advice, unfortunately, did not make it into much of his writing, and it took me a long time to learn the lesson.

Brandchaft (1993) has gone a step further and suggests we also focus on process, the conditions under which a particular affect arises. Fear, sadness, disappointment, frustration, rage, excitement, pride, accomplishment, or any other emotional response will arise in the context of a relational experience or, based on the past, an anticipated relational experience. The emotional response may then take on automatic meanings learned from those experiences.

Brandchaft gives the example of Marco, a writer who experienced depression after any success. Systematic investigation of the events immediately preceding each experience of depression helped Marco become aware that, when successful, he experienced an initial flush of pride and excitement. This enthusiasm then shifted, automatically and without awareness, into a profound sadness. Marco had only been aware of the depression, not of the process leading up to it. As Marco became aware of this process, of these automatic shifts in feelings, he remembered:

When he was twelve, he wrote the school play and asked his mother to come to watch on the night it was being performed. He wanted so for her to be pleased and proud, but she sat there unmoved and unimpressed. When he was introduced on the stage at the end of the play and the audience applauded, Marco noticed that his mother's hands remained fixed at her sides. . . .

Marco remained compelled to continue to experience as his very own his mother's sadness at his early interests, which took him away from her. . . . Marco's triumph at the opening of his play was being reflected back to him as an example of naughtiness, and he was responding as if he had no mind, no will, no credible experience of his own. [pp. 217–218]

To protect the vital connection with his mother, Marco learned at an early age to ward off feelings of pride and enthusiasm because feeling proud would hurt his mother. When he became aware of this process, of these voices from the past still operative within him, he was able to develop new relationships in which his pride and enthusiasm were met with validating, not painful, responses. He found his voice.

After many repetitions, early experiences of relationships organize into unconscious expectations. Children who are used to being treated with respect and support will come to expect, and feel they deserve, respect and support. Children who are used to rejection, criticism, and humiliation will believe that is what they deserve and what they should expect. They assume that if parents generally respond in a certain way, then that is how things are supposed to be.

These assumptions develop into automatic, unconscious ways of experiencing relationships, into organizing principles (Atwood and Stolorow 1984) or model scenes (Lichtenberg 1989). Marco, for example, became aware that one of his unconscious organizing principles was that taking care of himself hurt his mother. In the transference he struggled with unconscious feelings that he should organize himself around taking care of his analyst's needs. He believed the analyst needed him to come on time and was hurt every time Marco came late to his session. As the analyst confronted and interpreted this reaction, and helped Marco become aware of it and understand its origins in his early relationships, Marco became able to start developing a new organizing principle, a new way to experience a relationship. He felt he had a right to meet his needs and to take pride in his successes without having to worry that he would lose the connection with or hurt his analyst.

Bringing order to the unfolding of clinical material can help analysts make sense of patients' experiences. Making sense of patients' experiences and illuminating their unconscious organizing principles help patients develop their capacity for reflective self-awareness. They can begin to catch themselves reacting in old ways, make sense of their reactions, and start reacting in new ways. They learn self-reflection from the analyst's mode of inquiry and, over time, they develop the capacity for awareness on their own.

11

What Price
Survival?

A drowning man will catch at a straw.

English proverb

What follows is a psychoanalysis in detail with attention to the introspective-empathic mode of investigation, selfobject functioning, and process.

PRESENTING PROBLEM

Alan is a 28-year-old attorney who entered analysis because of depression and difficulty getting along with superiors. Early in the analysis his depression lifted, he got along better with employers, and, after one year, he moved to a new location to pursue a career opportunity. There he continued with another analyst, one who worked in a classical mode, as I did during that period.

Six years later he returned, successful in his career, happily married, and planning to start a family. He also was addicted to cocaine. He resumed his analysis with me, and this period lasted five years, the first two years of which centered on the cocaine addiction.

PAST HISTORY

Alan is the oldest of three children with a sister three years younger and a brother six years younger. His mother, a home-maker and schoolteacher, died of cancer at age 57, shortly after Alan's first year of analysis. He described his father, an engineer, as a "nice guy" but too "dependent" on mother. His father died of a heart attack at age 69, during the fourth year of our work together. His sister is a professional woman, and his brother, who had a psychotic break at age 19, lives in a board and care facility.

Alan began using cocaine after his mother's death and his first termination of analysis. Initially, he used the drug on week-ends for "recreation," but in time he used it daily and was addicted. Resolutions to stop the drug use were followed by periods of abstinence and then relapses. Intense self-disgust and feelings of failure accompanied each relapse. During this two-year period of drug use, he felt stuck, blamed himself, and anticipated that I would be fed up and disgusted with him.

Being conscientious, he routinely worked long hours, and when he got home late, he used cocaine to unwind. The drug dissolved all feelings of guilt, and he felt free and elated. Stimulated, he stayed up late and needed tranquilizers to sleep. The next morning in session he was tired and "hung over" from the tranquilizers. Hour after hour he came in tired and withdrawn, and castigated himself for being so "resistant" and wasting time. He felt certain that I was disappointed in him for "acting out" and for not "free associating better."

TRANSFERENCE

During these relapses, when he would put himself down and feel like a failure, I felt that he was protecting himself from painful interpretations that I had made in our previous work. By putting himself down first, pre-emptively, he could avoid the humiliation of feeling put down by me. Now my interpretations changed, and instead of focusing on content, on his behavior, I focused on process, the invisible links leading to his behavior. I looked for precipitating events.

Each time he told me that he used cocaine, I would ask him what had been going on in his life just before the drug use. He might reply that it was a Friday afternoon after a long, hard week, and driving home, he would think about cocaine and feel impatient to get high. I asked if he could recall his thoughts while driving home, and he could. He said he was anticipating the chores that needed doing and the demands that his wife would be making. He felt overwhelmed by pressures and responsibilities, and like a drowning man catching at a straw, he reached for cocaine. When he took the drug, he felt free from the responsibility to take care of everybody, and protected from the guilt he felt when he did something for himself.

Alan always anticipated the demands of others, and he felt responsible for everybody's happiness. He was always under pressure, yet he was not aware of feeling pressure. This was his normal state, what he was used to. Believing it was his job to make everything right before he could relax, he felt overwhelmed, and that was the precipitant.

During sessions when he felt exhausted and wanted to sleep, he felt guilty and apologized for not doing "more analysis." He anticipated that I expected more from him, and he put himself down to protect himself from my humiliating interpretations. I used the introspective-empathic mode and said that it was hard for him to take time to relax, rest, and recuperate, either by himself or in the presence of someone who would understand. Feeling understood provided him a validating selfobject experience.

This mode of understanding led to previously unavailable memories of past accomplishments both at school and at home. No matter how well he did, he recalled, his perfectionistic mother would point out more that could be done. His conscientious father had tedious chores for him to do such as weeding the lawn and carefully trimming the hedges. Although he worked hard and was conscientious, he remembered being called "lazy" if he took a break or wanted to watch TV instead of doing more work. To be able to come to his hour, to relax, to take care of his own needs and not have to perform, and to still feel that I was with him, was something new. He was beginning to experience a new way of relating where he could be himself and still feel connected.

COUNTERTRANSFERENCE

I reacted to his distance and withdrawal with countertransference feelings of frustration and impatience. I tried to engage him, in part to meet my selfobject needs for acknowledgment, and instead ended up retraumatizing him. I inadvertently became involved in reliving his early experiences where his parents expected him to meet *their* needs for engagement while *his* needs for comforting or for acknowledgment were either not recognized or were discounted.

When I understood my reactions and could be patient with him, I appreciated how, from his perspective, using the drug helped him. I did not condone using drugs, but I could appreciate that he was conscientious, worked hard, and took his responsibilities seriously. At the end of a week he needed a way to restore himself, to recharge his energies for another grueling week. I explained that because of blocks in aspects of his self-development, he had not yet developed efficient mechanisms for restoring himself, and had not yet learned how to turn to others for soothing or comfort. He felt that needing comfort was a sign of defect or weakness. Cocaine was expensive and caused him depression and fatigue, but it was the only way he knew to get around the guilt and isolation, to restore himself, and to prepare for the demands that would be made on him in the following week. When I told him he used the drug to survive, that got his attention. "You are fighting for survival and no one takes you seriously," he said. "People think you take it voluntarily and for pleasure—not for survival. It seems you have to be psychotic before your problems are taken seriously."

RESOLUTION

With this understanding and these new experiences, he became able to give himself permission to take time to soothe and restore himself. He read mystery novels, which relaxed him, and watched movies without feeling lazy. Although he acknowledged that his addiction was beyond his control, he felt shame at the idea of getting help. In the transference he anticipated that I expected him to handle the problem by himself. He also worried that I would be angry and jealous if he consulted an addiction specialist and did not rely solely on me. He believed that consulting a specialist would be disloyal to me. Clarification of this belief led to memories of long talks with his mother on "adult" topics. He could maintain her interest by being a good listener, but he noticed that his father was excluded and would withdraw. He felt anxious and guilty, believing that to show interest in his father would be disloyal to his mother and would upset her. He was supposed to need only her.

He then met weekly with a reputable addiction specialist, from whom he learned much. The doctor outlined a program that was initially helpful, but Alan soon began to disagree with some of his suggestions. The doctor was authoritarian, yet Alan could now assert himself and still maintain rapport. He followed those suggestions that were helpful, and declined those that were not. It was a new experience for him to feel an alliance with the doctor while maintaining his own feeling of individuality.

DEPRESSION

Alan felt stronger, became more confident, and finally stopped using drugs, but he also became aware of deep feelings of emptiness, and became depressed. Previously warded-off, painful feelings from earlier experiences were now emerging. These were the feelings of isolation, emptiness, despair, and hopelessness that had been disavowed in childhood because they seemed dangerous. He not only felt isolated and frightened, but felt there was something wrong with him for feeling that way. Alan's new integration made it possible for him to begin using me to process those early experiences. I viewed his depression as a sign of progress, not illness.

During this period of depression, I found Alan less withdrawn and easier to engage than when he was using cocaine. Our connection grew stronger, and on those occasions when he had relapses and used the drug, he was surprised to find that it had lost its appeal. Now he had other resources for dealing with tensions—he had conquered his addiction.

The second phase of the analysis focused on his depression and on increasing marital tension. The cocaine made it easy to disavow the painful feelings, but now he became aware of his isolation and loneliness. More engaged with me, he felt encouraged to try to engage his wife in a more intimate relationship. That attempt upset a balance that had developed between them, and he struggled with feelings of frustration and disappointment in his marriage. If he tried to assert himself with his wife, they fought. If he tried to placate her, he felt defeated. Talking to me helped him resolve these tensions, and his marriage improved. His struggle then moved into the transference.

The focus of the transference shifted from a primarily self-object dimension, where he felt understood and safe, to the conflictual dimension. He complained that he felt pressure from me to perform like he felt with his wife. He felt that I was disgusted with him for being late to sessions, for not free associating properly, for not having transference reactions to me, and for not remembering more from his past.

He believed that if he did not perform, I would get fed up, withdraw, and leave him to fend for himself. Illumination of these fears led to memories of his mother's isolation and withdrawal when she felt overwhelmed. He had not realized that she had limitations but had assumed that her emotional distance was his fault for not taking better care of her. This feeling of responsibility was revived when his brother had a psychotic break. Alan felt that his competitive feelings had caused his brother's condition. He recalled how he and his brother had established a close relationship that was cut short by the psychotic break, and felt intense grief for the loss of that relationship. As he worked through and resolved feelings of responsibility for his mother's cancer, he experienced intense grief for that loss as well.

He had been blocked in his ability to feel and to process painful feelings. This block was due in part to disavowal, to his walling off feelings to protect the relationship with his parents because he saw their distress when he was in pain. The block was also due in part to an arrest in affect integration, the result of a lack of attuned responsiveness from his parents in his early years. His parents had difficulty helping him develop a vocabulary for the awareness and expression of painful feelings. His new ability to integrate these painful feelings made possible the mourning of his losses and, as a result, he felt stronger, better integrated, and more confident.

He became bolder in the transference and complained about me. He had heard that I was a self psychologist who was different from the other analysts and who did not believe in interpreting aggression. He worried that he was being short-changed in his analysis. Tuning in to his affect, not the literal complaints, I asked if he feared that his complaints or disappointments in me would hurt me, an unconscious organizing principle. "Yes," he said. "You will be hurt and withdraw from me." The illumination of this belief in the transference led to painful memories of Mother's withdrawal from him when he disappointed her. His anxiety to perform and to be good for her, he realized, was a desperate attempt to protect himself from the frightening feelings of isolation that he suffered when she was unhappy and withdrew from him.

I interpreted his dilemma: either he did what was expected and complied to maintain a necessary tie, in which case he felt like a servant or a slave, or he stood up for himself and rebelled, in which case he was labeled a troublemaker. That fit for him, and he had always assumed that was how it was supposed to be. He recalled a memory where his mother had asked him to drown some newborn kittens. Although this was an accepted practice in their rural community, neither Mother nor Father was willing to do it. When he protested, his mother pressured him, and he complied. He had assumed that there was something wrong with him for being squeamish, and it did not occur to him that he had a right to protest.

With this new self-awareness, he felt relief from pressures to please his wife at all costs. He became able to be assertive without humiliating her and to be loving without demeaning himself. He took time off to pursue his interests, and he experienced more energy for family and friends.

In the sessions he became stiff and uneasy, but he did not say anything—a sign of resistance to the emergence of transference. One way an analyst can provide an attuning selfobject function is by focusing on tension states that are not verbalized. I inquired, "You seem tense talking about this. Are you feeling some tension? Does that fit for you?" Alan said, "I hadn't realized it, but now that you mention it, I do feel tense. Yes, that's the word—tense." He was having doubts about me, but to even be aware of them was dangerous. His awareness of his feelings, he believed, made him disloyal to me or hurt me, and that was dangerous. That was his resistance.

With the interpretation of this resistance, he realized that he worried about my being a "wimp" when I did not respond to his criticisms, and when I did not stand up to him and defend myself. He felt disappointed in me and he was frightened. When he saw that I was not hurt by his disappointment, he felt safer. More transference feelings then emerged. He had heard other stories about me: that I believed in being "nice," that I was afraid of my "unresolved aggression." Previously I would have understood that he was afraid of his anger toward me, but now I saw that he felt vulnerable, and I interpreted his fear that he could not count on me, that I would not be strong enough to be a good role model for him and help him develop his assertiveness. With relief and humor, he said, "I guess you couldn't be too much of a wimp. You raised my fee last year and you complain when I don't pay my bill!" Feeling stronger, he remembered feeling frightened by his father's passivity and that he had wanted his father to be more assertive.

Alan recalled that his mother complained to him about her disappointment in his father, and I asked if he felt that closeness with his father would be disloyal to his mother. That fit for him and clarified another unconscious organizing principle: closeness to Father would hurt his mother. With this insight, he remembered fishing trips with his father, times when he felt close to him and special. He had disavowed those feelings of closeness because it would jeopardize his relationship with his mother, and he could not be close to both of them.

Feeling renewed longings for closeness with his father, Alan called him, and they arranged a trip. His father's warmth and openness surprised him, and they re-established their relationship.

Alan felt pleased that he was changing, but an emerging transference theme worried him: he was becoming too much like me and was losing his identity. His unconscious organizing principle was that if he developed interests or had opinions that were different from mine, I would withdraw my support. He had to be like me and had to depend on me. He had a dream: he was climbing a hill, going up a gravel road; there was a power station at the top of the hill. It was like a prison and was patrolled by dogs. Then he saw another power station on a golf course. In the analysis of the dream I was the first power station, a function that I provided. To rely on me and my power was to be imprisoned, an expression of his compliance. He realized that he was discovering a source of power within himself, the second power station. He could assert himself, say no, and still feel connected. He hired a gardener and used the time saved to renew his interest in golf, a longtime passion of his and not mine.

TERMINATION

The feeling that he was changing and becoming his own person introduced the termination phase. He realized that he did not have to be like me, that he could choose those aspects of me he wanted to emulate and reject others. He alternated between feeling ready to terminate and feeling that there must be more to do. He recalled his father's ambitious projects that could never be completed. He felt unsure of his judgment, and wanted me to make the decision to terminate. He recalled his mother being worried that he would embarrass her by making wrong choices. Mother knew what was best, and she did not tolerate mistakes. Mistakes were shameful failures, and were not viewed as opportunities to learn. Alan had learned very early to discount his intuitions and do things his mother's way.

Trusting himself now, he announced that he wanted to terminate in six months, at the end of our fifth year. He worried about my response as he expected me to say either that he had more work to do or that he should be done already. We explored both fears and then set a termination date.

He reacted to the date with renewed feelings of sadness for the losses of his mother, his father, his brother, and me. He reported a dream in which he missed his appointment because his clock was all messed up. He was distracted with other things and forgot to come. He felt a sense of loss but also a sense of guilt. "I didn't pay attention," he said. The dream illustrated an organizing principle, a process where a feeling of loss was automatically and unconsciously translated into a meaning of failure. If he felt a loss, he must have done something wrong; if he paid more attention, losses would not occur.

He thought about our relationship and the fact that I did not tell him what to do or tell him to stop using cocaine. I helped him to become aware of his feelings, his tensions and fears. Now he felt free of pressure to take care of others first. He said, "I feel like I'm saying good-bye."

He alternated between fear of giving me up as a source of support and pride in his new strength and confidence. He then worried that I would think he was bragging when he felt proud of himself. He recalled his father telling him not to show off, that he was too big for his britches. He also recalled Mother's anxiety when he was pleased and excited, and how she would admonish him to "get hold of yourself." As he felt more separate from me, he became acutely aware of how enmeshed he had been with his mother.

As the termination date approached, he told me that he felt guilty about being a better father than his father and about making more money than I did. He believed that anything he got was always at somebody else's expense. "There are days now when I see things really clearly," he said, "when I can figure things out for myself."

He was pleased that he could now think about what was best for him without worrying about its impact on me. He felt appreciation for our relationship, which he said had sustained him. A turning point in his struggle to give up cocaine was when he first felt that the analysis was for him and not for me.

In the last hour he looked forward to pursuing the analysis on his own. He felt grateful, but he worried if I would be all right, if I could survive without him. He recalled his fears that his father would not be all right, especially after his mother died, but now he realized that his father was strong. He thought about how far he had come; he didn't even think about drugs anymore. He felt confident and sad. I said that I had changed and had learned from him, too, and we hugged and said good-bye.

In summary, this case illustrates:

- The introspective-empathic mode of investigation, looking at Alan's use of drugs from the vantage point of his experience.
- The concept of selfobject functioning, attuning to affect states and helping him develop a vocabulary for those affects.
- Focus on process, illuminating the precipitants of behavior, the mechanisms by which experiences translate into meanings.

My appreciation of his struggle to overcome irrational feelings of responsibility and to complete an arrested self-individuation process allowed him to change from a compliance-or-rebellion stance to one of intimacy and healthy assertion. In the transference I was experienced as providing selfobject functions and as repeating painful experiences. My focus on process allowed for the unfolding, illumination, and transformation of his unconscious organizing principles.

12

Patients
without Mercy

The necessity of the times ... calls for circumspection, deliberation, fortitude and perseverance.

Samuel Adams

Patients who were abused and molested as children will, at some point in every successful analysis, feel abused and molested by the analyst, and the analyst will feel abused and molested by the patient. These patients are people for whom pain or suffering is necessary in order to experience a human connection.

ORGANIZING PRINCIPLES

In the past, these patients were labeled as masochistic because it was believed that internal instinctual pressures or aggressive wishes turned inward motivated their behavior (Brenner 1959; Freud 1919, 1923). Self psychology now understands that this self-destructive behavior is based on unconscious organizing principles or model scenes that have developed in the context of early relationships.

For example, a small child with an uninvolved mother and an abusive father will turn to the abusing father for support because turning to the unavailable mother results in no emotional connection. A painful connection is preferable to isolation, and suffering abuse is the price that must be paid to feel the security of a connection. A patient reported a dream in which her face was swollen and painful. She consulted a doctor who treated her, but he was cruel and rough with her, and he was insulting. "I had no choice," she said. "I was in pain and I needed help." Her experience of relationships had become organized into a belief that pain was a condition of support. As adults in analysis, these patients have not yet learned that one can stay connected with others in the absence of pain.

DEVELOPMENT

In normal development, the stronger the bond between a mother and her developing infant, the greater the tension during the developing toddler's self-individuation. Much of the tension during the "terrible twos" results from the toddler's need to assert individuality yet maintain a human connection. Mothers of healthy 2-year-olds report feeling overwhelmed, as if they are being overrun by ruthless monsters. Even so, they admire and take pride in their children's budding self-assertiveness and individuality.

A mother wants to help her distressed child, but often finds herself in a no-win position. If she is calm and soothing, the child may become tyrannical; if she is firm, the child may feel betrayed and unloved. Her task at such times is to survive and to stay connected to her child without feeling destroyed by the child or retaliating and destroying the child. If she can manage to get through the year, a wonderful change takes place at age 3. The "terrible two" transforms into a "tender three." Similar struggles are experienced between parents and normal adolescents.

Because some parents must have compliance, a child may be deprived of the opportunity to be a normal 2-year-old. A mother might give the message that she is hurt or damaged by the child's pulling away, and the child comes to believe that self-assertion will destroy or irreparably harm the mother. The mother might feel overwhelmed and become punitive toward the child, and the child comes to believe that self-assertion results in retaliatory violence. These children learn at a very early age either to be compliant, to be "good" and do what is expected, or to withdraw and keep their distance. As a result, much of their self-assertiveness and self-individuation is derailed.

SURVIVAL

In their analyses as adults, these patients will try to engage the analyst at this point in their development and to use the analyst to provide the experience of a benignly opposing force that supports active opposition and confirms a sense of individuality (Wolf 1988). Wolf calls this an *adversarial selfobject function*. In other words, these patients relive the "terrible twos," and during this phase of an analysis, sessions are stormy; analysts struggle to keep their balance. The task of the analyst during this phase is, like the parent of a 2-year-old, to survive and not be destroyed by the patient, and not to make retaliatory interpretations that make the patient feel destroyed (Shapiro 1989).

Patients who were deprived of the opportunity to be a "terrible two" also report repeated painful experiences, such as humiliation, neglect, isolation, or physical abuse, that leave them constantly feeling small, weak, helpless, and afraid. Compounding their trauma is a lack of the attuned responsiveness from caregivers necessary to help the child process and overcome the painful feelings.

In their analyses as adults, these patients will subject the analyst to tests. Identifying with traumatizing parents, these patients will sense the analyst's areas of vulnerability and subtly provoke the analyst into feeling small, weak, helpless, humiliated, and ashamed. An example is the patient who, sensing my need to be helpful, started complaining that I was making her worse, not better. As a girl she felt abused and unappreciated by her mother, and now I began to feel abused and unappreciated by her. My feeling abused, however, did not lead to help-lessness, but became an opportunity for analytic work.

COUNTERTRANSFERENCE

Analysts who feel abused by their patients often feel abused by colleagues and supervisors who tell them they should remain calm. In traditional analysis, analysts are supposed to remain neutral. In the traditional model, feeling angry with or feeling defeated by patients is evidence of unresolved conflict in the analyst. This attitude is reflected by Brenner (1959). From a traditional stance, Brenner suggests that the analyst maintain a condition in which "the analyst is not himself unconsciously tempted to participate with the patient in . . . sadomasochistic behavior: to become angry at the patient, to feel hopeless and defeated by him, or to demonstrate either affection or aversion in whatever way" (p. 223). Brenner advised:

> A model of behavior for the analyst to follow is that of an understanding adult . . . dealing reasonably with a sulky, stubborn, provocative child. If the adult is wise and not unduly involved emotionally with the child, he is not upset or disturbed by such a child's behavior but remains calmly observant and understanding whatever may be the child's attempts to seduce and provoke him into a sadomasochistic episode. . . . this is easier said than done but . . . it is not impossible, and . . . is essential to the optimal analytic treatment of the masochistic patient. [p. 224]

No involved adult, in my opinion, can remain calm and under-standing in the face of a healthy child's provocative behavior, such as that of a normal 2-year-old or a vigorous adolescent. And no matter how understanding analysts are, at some point they will become angry at their patients, and they will feel hope-less and defeated by them. It is too much to ask of analysts that they always remain calm and objective in the face of these provocations.

The successful analyst is one who can survive the onslaught. The temptation is either to be defensive and explain or justify one's position, or to make interpretations and explain the patient's motivations. Either tactic may lead to a disruption. Being defensive may make the patient feel anxious; explaining the patient's behavior may make the patient feel criticized or guilty. Doing neither and weathering the storm, feeling hurt by the patient or angry at the patient and getting over it without feeling guilty or blaming the patient, sets the recovery process in motion.

Patients become able to allow themselves, in identification with their analysts, more leeway in experiencing a broad range of affects. They begin overcoming those identifications with their overwhelmed, traumatizing parents and start identifying with their analysts' strengths. Patients realize that their analysts can get upset and recover by themselves without making the patient responsible, and these patients come to believe there is hope for them, too. They consider the possibility of being hurt and of recovering without having to feel small, helpless, and vulnerable. They can complain, express their painful feelings, and count on being understood and taken seriously. These new experiences help them to begin integrating and overcoming early traumatic experiences and to begin developing new organizing principles.

Analysts who can survive these assaults without either feeling destroyed or making interpretations that leave the patient feeling destroyed can use their countertransference feelings as opportunities for furthering the analytic process. In the past I saw these assaults on me as evidence of underlying instinctual wishes needing to be tamed or neutralized. Now I see these behaviors as attempts to use me to complete an arrested phase of development and to master early traumatic experiences. In time the patient may become curious about these behaviors, and I will make an interpretation and explain my understanding of the process, but some patients will feel stronger and move on to new areas without needing an interpretation.

The analyst who is patient and understanding will sometimes become frightening to these patients once a bond has been established. As patients feel closer and safer, they may feel vulnerable to loss and disappointment. The more understanding the analyst is, the more anxious these patients become. They believe unconsciously that no pain means no connection (Stolorow 1975). If they can experience the analyst as abusive, they feel hurt, but safe.

What can you do when your patient experiences you as abusive? Theoretically you remain objective and investigate your patient's experience, but practically, that does not work. Your patient knows you too well, and there will be some element of truth in your patient's perception of you.

A useful approach is described by Lichtenberg and colleagues (1992) in which the analyst accepts and then explores the patient's attributions. The analyst, Lichtenberg says, "wears the attribution":

> To use this method successfully, analysts must be conceptually and emotionally open to the pain (and sometimes joy) of discovering aspects of themselves they may only be dimly aware of (or defensively unaware of). With the analyst's encouragement, the patient is invited to enter with the analyst into an investigation of the attitude under question—what the analyst has done to trigger the attribution at this time, how the patient responds to the analyst's annoyance or criticism, where their values converge (I think we are both greedy) or diverge, and what meaning these convergences and divergences have. [p. 192]

CASE EXAMPLES

Jane was depressed following the breakup of her marriage. She felt helpless and frightened, and she complained that I did not understand her. I tried harder to understand her, but she became more despairing. Then she reported a dream: "I came to the office and your door was open. When I looked in, you were sitting in your chair and holding a baby in your lap."

Exploring the dream revealed that she felt I was treating her like a baby. I was trying too hard to help her and she felt infantilized. I acknowledged that I had not trusted her and could see how that would scare her. I relaxed and she complained that I could not understand her and that she felt hopeless. Continued investigation revealed how anxious her mother would become when Jane complained, especially after her father died. She felt despair and hopelessness then, but she had been deprived of the opportunity to talk about and master the painful feelings. Now she was using me to help process the pain and the feelings of vulnerability.

When I tried to "fix" her and relieve her pain, I was like her anxious mother, and she felt more hopeless and alone. When I "let her suffer" and complain about me, she felt stronger and remembered more about her painful loss. Although the dream may have represented unconscious wishes to have me treat her like a baby, that was not what she was feeling. More convincing was the idea that the dream represented her perception of a countertransference attitude of which I was not aware. Investigating her perception of me exposed her translation of my infantilizing attitude into a sign of her inadequacy. It had not occurred to her that I could have limitations. My "wearing the attribute" and recognizing the element of truth encoded in her perception, and discussing it with her, helped her to overcome the belief that other people's anxieties (her mother's, her former husband's, and mine) were reflections of her failings.

Here are excerpts from an hour of my work with Mary where, by provoking my vulnerability and seeing me survive, she began to overcome her feeling of vulnerability:

Mary consulted me at age 28 because of severe depression. Sexually molested in early childhood by an older brother, by her stepfather when she was 12, and by her uncle when she was

19, she reported a series of stormy, painful adult relationships. After one year of analysis she entered a relationship with Bob, a gentle, warm, and loving man. Mary repeatedly found herself being short with him, criticizing and provoking him. Although he felt hurt and mystified by her outbursts, he patiently waited for her to calm down and they then resolved their differences. This made Mary more anxious, however, because it was harder for her to feel connected with him when he was calm.

I had a taste of Bob's experience when Mary began one session glaring at me, and said, "I'm in a dangerous mood." I waited for her to continue, but she just sat silently. (We met face to face.) Then she began to complain bitterly, "I'm tired of always regretting everything I do." She explained that she could not control her outbursts of temper at Bob, following which she always felt ashamed. I felt she was having a temper outburst at me.

She railed loudly at me, detailing her frustrations, her disappointments, and her feelings of shameful failure. I felt the criticisms were directed at me, and I felt guilty and defensive as though I had not done my job. She was nailing me where I was most vulnerable, and I lost my balance.

Normally in such a situation, I would reflect back and understand her feelings of disappointment, frustration, and discouragement, but having lost my bearings, I found myself saying, "Are you angry with me?" Although that was accurate since she was clearly angry, that was not central to her self-experience at that moment. She was feeling overwhelmed and disconnected, and she was struggling to reconnect with me.

She shot back: "No, I'm not angry at you—it's myself I hate!" Then more loudly: "I can't continue going through life like this! I have to get a handle on myself!" I waited. She looked at me and yelled, "I'm really pissed at you!" When I continued to wait, she shouted at me, "Why am I still so fat! Why am I still blowing up? So I'm successful at work, but that's not my top priority! I want to be able to get along with people!"

I felt pressured by her intensity, found myself withdrawing from her, and became passive and silent. She looked directly at me and zeroing in on my point of maximum vulnerability, she yelled, "You know what's wrong with me! You just won't tell me! I have to do everything for myself! You just sit there and don't do anything!" I stayed silent and, feeling guilty and inadequate, became even more withdrawn. Then she shouted at me, "What's wrong with me, Dr. Shapiro, why do I behave like this?" Still off balance, I felt I had to say something to get out of my shell and reconnect with her. I answered weakly, "I don't know." She said sarcastically, "Why don't you know? You're supposed to know." Regaining my balance, I said in an echoing fashion, "I should know." "Yes," she said, "you're the almighty expert!"

My withdrawal had scared her and she became anxious and ashamed and began putting herself down: "I shouldn't get so upset. I shouldn't complain. I should be nice. I should be appreciative." But now I was back on track, and I interpreted her defense, her putting herself down to protect herself from anticipated criticism. "Is that what you feel," I asked, "or is that what you believe I am thinking about you?" That reassured her and galvanized her. Her timid anxiety disappeared and, in a bold, strong manner she said, "You don't care! It doesn't make any difference to you!" Staying with her affect, her experience, I said, "You feel I'm indifferent." "Yes," she said, "I'm so ugly and you don't even care." Feeling concern, I asked her if I had indicated in some way that I saw her as ugly. She said, "No, but you wouldn't tell me if you did." I now felt in tune with her feelings and said, "But you expect that I am put off by you, that I'm not pleased that you're able to be more assertive with me and speak up for yourself."

That touched her, and she became sad. "I don't have any impact on you," she said. I answered, "I'm just indifferent to you. I don't care." Tears welled up, and she began to cry, and she said, "I always feel better, more calm, when I'm able to express myself in here."

She told me about her weekend with Bob. It was his birthday, but she felt furious with him and struggled to keep control of her temper. She did not feel like making love and, finally, she was able to talk to him. "Everything came out," she said, "and I felt much better. I just wish I didn't get so upset with him," she said, feeling frustrated and ashamed. I said it was a struggle for her to talk about feelings of anger and disappointment, that she feared hurting people and driving them away, and added, "But you seem to be learning to express angry feelings in here with me." She said, "I would rather be angry with you than with Bob." "It's hard," I said, "when you anticipate that the other person will be put off or hurt." "I just sound so much like my mother," she said, "it really pisses me off." I asked, "Is that also scary?" She said, "It makes me feel absolutely hopeless. I don't understand why it keeps happening." The hour ended.

This hour illustrates Mary's attempts to use me in her recovery from the effects of early abuse. The therapeutic task was twofold:

- She felt strong enough internally and safe enough with me to begin the painful process of disengaging from feelings of enmeshment with me and completing her self-individuation.
- She needed to test me, to exploit my feelings of vulnerability, to get control and to master her own feelings of vulnerability.

In this hour, Mary felt safe enough to berate me with criticisms.

When I withdrew, she became anxious, and began putting herself down. When I interpreted her defense and helped her make sense of her experience without blaming her, we reconnected. Previously warded-off feelings of sadness then came into awareness. Feeling her sadness in my presence was a poignantly close moment between us, and it strengthened her.

In another case I had to rely on intuition, on emotional hunches, when a lack of experience and training left me facing a desperate situation. A young professional woman, Jill entered analysis because of recurrent depression and angry outbursts at co-workers. Eight years earlier she had tried to kill herself by cutting her neck with a razor.

The first two years of the analysis went well. Jill's depression lifted as she expressed disappointment and resentment over her father's rigidity and controlling behavior. In the third year, she began to recall her mother's emotional distance and unavailability, and realized that much of her early emotional support came from her grandmother.

Painful feelings emerged, and Jill often thrashed about on the couch in distress, unable to find words to express herself. When I asked if she felt frightened or fragmented, she relaxed. Finding words to fit with her feelings was an integrating experience for her, and as long as I could come up with the right words, she would feel relief; but I did not understand what caused her distress, nor did I know how to help her move beyond it.

At that point in my development I understood her difficulty as the result of a regression, a retreat to an earlier stage of emotional development. I believed the regression was a normal psychoanalytic process arising from forces within her and had nothing to do with me. I expected that patience and understanding, plus appropriate interpretations, would move her beyond the regression into a new experience of insight, strength, and integration.

At that time I did not understand about process, about the experiences that precipitate fragmentation experiences, so I did not inquire into the precipitants of her regressive experiences. In particular, I did not inquire about what contributions I had made. Although painful feelings from early experiences were now being stirred up (I prefer to call this a deepening of the analysis and not a regression), she was also having more difficulty feeling connected with me. Cut off from visual cues, my silence during her struggles left her feeling alone and unconnected, but when I could comment on her feelings, she felt reconnected with me and reintegrated within herself.

When I did not know what to say, I remained silent, and she felt I was not there. It did not occur to me to tell her I didn't know what to say so she would at least feel I was present. At one point, her feeling of disconnection led to a breakdown.

It happened during an hour where she was unable to talk, and I felt anguish and confusion as I watched her struggle and I felt helpless as she became more agitated. I thought that something would eventually occur to me, but she couldn't stand it any longer, and without a word, she got up and started to walk out.

I have had patients walk out, come back the next day, and talk about it; but this scared me. If Jill walked out I expected I would never see her again. As she opened the door, I said, "Wait, please." None of my rules was working, and I was operating on pure intuition. Jill returned and sat at the foot of the couch with her back to me. I felt I had only a moment to act before she would leave again.

I was in turmoil. I wanted to be helpful, yet I feared I would make a technical error and ruin everything. My reasoning processes failed me, but my intuition came to the rescue. I suddenly had a strong image of myself sitting next to her on the couch. Without thinking, I got up and went to her, sat next to her, and put my arm around her.

I had never before touched a patient during a session. For one thing it was against the "rules," and for another it was foreign to my reserved nature, but I held Jill and she relaxed. Neither of us talked, but I felt our connection was re-established. Five minutes later the hour ended, and I said, "We'll continue next time." She nodded and left, and the next day she resumed the analysis as if nothing had happened.

Over the next six months we talked much about the experience. We both felt that my reaching out to her and holding her helped us get through a difficult period where neither of us had the words to connect with each other. That situation never recurred.

The analysis ultimately progressed to a successful conclusion. Jill's depression resolved, her career flourished, and she married and raised a family. Five years after termination she came to see me to say good-bye. Her husband was being transferred, and she was continuing her career in the new community. Her children were doing well, and she was pleased. We talked about the hour when I held her, and she remembered it exactly as I did, and said, "I was really out of it. I don't know what would have happened to me if I had left then."

Since then I have learned to be more sensitive to a patient's feeling of disconnection and to my role in the process. Being aware of more factors helps, but we are always learning and there will always be desperate situations to deal with. For a long time I saw my behavior as a failure and I felt ashamed. Even though the results were positive, I never told anyone about the experience because I expected to be criticized. But it was not a failure, it was a success. It was also an example of the power of the rules I had learned.

13

Couples
Therapy

*Couples are wholes and not wholes, what agrees disagrees,
the concordant is discordant. From all things one and from
one all things.*

Heraclitus

Couples therapy is like individual therapy in some ways and
unlike it in others. At times I feel I am doing therapy with
one or the other of the partners as I would in individual therapy;
at other times I feel I am doing therapy with the couple as a
unit. I can also be an observer watching the partners help each
other.

Self psychology enriches couples therapy in two ways:

- It helps partners to decenter from their own point of view and
  to empathically investigate the experiences of another. This
  leads to a better understanding and a decrease in tension between the partners.
- It helps partners understand the role of selfobject functioning in both normal and troubled relationships. This results
  in partners becoming more giving to each other and more tolerant of disappointments in the relationship.

EMPATHIC INVESTIGATION

While similarities bring people together, dealing with each other's differences becomes the work of a relationship. Expressions of frustration or disappointment by one partner may translate into experiences of criticism or rejection by the other partner. The therapist's ability to decenter from a personal experience and, using the introspective-empathic mode, enter the experience of another provides a powerful role model for partners.

Dawn, a graduate student, came to see me with her husband Mike, an engineer. Dawn idealized her individual therapist, and she felt certain I could perform similar miracles for Mike. The problem, Dawn said, was that Mike was not interested in therapy.

Mike said he was happy with Dawn and he wished she would accept him for who he was and stop pressuring him to change. Dawn complained that Mike withdrew from her and isolated himself in his room with his computer, which made her feel hurt and rejected. He did not feel he was rejecting her, but he needed to do his work. He sensed Dawn's disappointment in him, and it made him feel like a failure as a husband. Dawn said that if he just had some therapy he "wouldn't be afraid of intimacy" and would stay "present" with her.

They argued back and forth and Dawn became loud and strident, while Mike grew quiet and withdrawn. I appreciated Dawn's frustration in wanting to feel more strongly connected to her husband and her anxiety when she experienced his withdrawal, her fear that he would not return to her. I also appreciated Mike's feeling of inadequacy and failure when his wife complained. Using the empathic mode of investigation, I alternately put myself into the experience of each of them, and in time they each began to emulate me. They became capable of sustained empathic investigation. They became able to understand the other person's point of view without feeling they had to agree with it.

TRANSFERENCE

As they started getting along better with each other, transference feelings emerged and Dawn turned on me. She told me she was in individual therapy, that therapy was good for her, and it would be good for Mike, too. Why didn't I tell him that? When I said that entering therapy was a personal decision, and that what was right for one person was not necessarily right for another, she exploded. "Don't you believe in therapy?" she demanded. "Yes," I said, "I believe in therapy." "Then why don't you recommend it for Mike? You would be a great therapist for him," she said.

I said that I appreciated her confidence, and I would be happy to work with Mike individually, if that was what he wanted, but Mike had made it clear that he was not interested, at least at this time. Mike then revealed that he experienced Dawn's pressure to go into therapy as an intrusion, as if she was trying to run his life, and if he did decide on therapy, he would prefer to go into group and not individual therapy. When I said that I had confidence in Mike's ability to know what was best for him, Dawn became furious. She felt betrayed by me. I had come highly recommended, and she was certain that I could "fix" her husband. When I said, understandingly, that I appreciated her disappointment in me, she became apoplectic. Screaming at me, she said that she was furious and felt like waiting outside for me to leave so she could slash the tires on my bicycle. As in individual therapy, I stayed with her experience and tried to appreciate her frustration and disappointment.

Mike, visibly shaken by Dawn's outburst, turned to me and said, "Doesn't that scare you?" "No," I said, "Dawn has a temper, she expresses herself, and then she gets over it. I appreciate her openness, but does this happen at home?" "Yes," Mike said, "she blows up like this all the time, and I don't know what to do except retreat to my study."

Now it became clear that Dawn expressed her frustrations

and disappointments in great emotional outbursts. "I have an Irish temper," she said, "but I get over it." Not trusting her to spontaneously wind down, Mike became frightened and protected himself by withdrawal. Dawn, not appreciating how scared Mike was, became anxious, believing that Mike was leaving her and would not come back. Feeling the loss as a personal rejection, as an abandonment, her anger escalated, and a vicious cycle ensued. Her anxiety over Mike's withdrawal resulted in more explosions. His anxiety resulted in more withdrawal.

With their new understanding of each other's fears, they were able to trust each other. Mike trusted that Dawn's outbursts would blow over, and Dawn trusted Mike to return from his retreat. They learned to be patient and more tolerant with each other. My staying calm and being understanding during Dawn's outburst served as a role model for Mike. He could identify with my calm and stay present with Dawn.

SELFOBJECT EXPERIENCES

Turning to partners for selfobject experiences such as soothing, comforting, validating, and strengthening is a part of all normal relationships. When your partner comes through for you and can furnish a selfobject experience, your sense of self is enhanced. When your partner disappoints you, a disruption in the self-selfobject bond occurs, and your self-esteem suffers. The more vulnerable you feel, the more difficulty you have in maintaining your internal feeling of cohesion.

Many of the tensions experienced by couples follow feelings of loss of self-cohesion—fragmentation or breakdown secondary to disappointment or frustration. These experiences range from mild, transient losses of self-esteem to disorganization with intense feelings of betrayal and violent rages. When a couple turns to the therapist to provide such selfobject experiences, similar tensions will emerge in the transference. Couples ultimately struggle with commonly shared selfobject experiences and, in the process, use each other to develop further. (This is an original idea of Richard F. Avery, LCSW.)

With one couple, Sam, a 34-year-old surgeon, and Colleen, a 36-year-old nurse, the therapy illustrates both selfobject and conflictual transferences operating between them, between each of them and me, and between them as a couple and me. Married for five years with two young children, they consulted me because, after years of bitter fighting, they felt hopeless. It was the first marriage for Sam, the son of a physician, who relied on his father for advice, and had ended an earlier relationship on the advice of his father when his fiancée developed diabetes. Colleen's first marriage ended in divorce after ten years, and she did not want to go through another divorce.

We met once a week for 90-minute sessions, and the therapy lasted three years. The first half of each session was spent in bitter fighting; they yelled, cursed, and insulted each other. The second half of the session was spent talking. At first I tried to curtail the fighting. I found it painful and frightening to watch, and I tried to interrupt their outbursts, to ask them to talk and to be rational, but as soon as one had a turn to speak, like the top blowing off a volcano, fire erupted. When I could contain my anxiety and trust them and the therapeutic process, I waited patiently and said little except to identify the hurt and the fear each was experiencing. Colleen felt hurt and humiliated by Sam's criticizing her publicly in front of family and friends. Sam felt terrified and vulnerable because of the way he saw Colleen spending money.

The fighting, I came to realize, served three functions: (1) Feeling safe with me, they discharged much of the tension that had built up during the week at home, where they avoided talking to each other and became estranged. (2) The fighting served as an organizing experience for them, a desperate, painful way of engaging each other. I provided a containing selfobject function, an environment where it was safe and they could fight and reconnect. (3) The fighting also served a communication function. They were showing me their desperation, the intensity of their betrayed feelings, and the depth of their despair. They anticipated that I would be critical of their fighting and try to stop them. Instead, I appreciated how frightened and desperate they were feeling. That surprised them as they had not thought of themselves as frightened or desperate.

My tuning in to their feelings of fear and desperation provided a selfobject experience for them. By helping them to identify and label those affects, they could begin to integrate the feelings and not feel so vulnerable. They had felt the marriage was hopeless and they would have to separate because they could not get along, a sign that their relationship was defective. Now they could talk about and get over their hopelessness, and they felt validated in their commitment to each other and to their relationship.

The therapy progressed in three phases. In the opening phase, lasting three months, they idealized me as I clarified their feelings and contained their anxiety. Sam felt that Colleen destroyed his freedom with complaints about his time away from home, and he felt diminished and pushed away when she called him selfish and immature. Colleen felt humiliated and enraged when Sam attacked and put her down in front of his family and her friends.

During this phase I helped them to understand about selfobject functioning:

- Each of them struggled with underlying feelings of vulnerability and looked to the other to provide a sense of safety.
- Each of them looked to the other to supply a selfobject strengthening function, to be someone who would not disappoint. The other's strength would compensate for what was felt to be lacking within.
- Feelings of disappointment in these areas were experienced as a personal betrayal, as an injury to the sense of self. It was like your car failing to start when you are counting on it to get you to an important meeting. And, I pointed out, rage is a normal reaction to feeling betrayed.

They now saw me as a source of strength on which they could count. Although they still did not like the way each was treated by the other, they did not feel so vulnerable and hope returned. This new feeling of hope ushered in the middle phase of the therapy, which lasted two years.

"We've been coming for three months now and we're still fighting. Nothing has happened," they complained. I noted to myself that they were finally doing something together, complaining about me, and that finally they were not fighting. A transference between them as a couple and me was emerging and, resonating with their experience, I simply said, "You're feeling disappointed."

I did not yet want to share my reaction of pleasure at their new togetherness because it would serve to discount their complaint, which I wanted to take seriously. I told them that I appreciated their letting me know about their disappointment in me, and I invited them to tell me more about their expectations and frustrations. As they spoke, I noticed that they were becoming tense, and I commented on it.

Exploration of their tension, which was so automatic that they were not aware of it, brought out the emerging transference fear that I would be hurt by their criticisms. As their complaints about me were taken seriously and understood, they began to take each other's complaints seriously, to hear and understand each other. My acknowledgment of their feelings helped them learn to provide acknowledging selfobject experiences for each other. New genetic material and memories of past experiences now spontaneously emerged. The course of the therapy was changing.

Sam realized, with a jolt, that his mother always discounted his feelings whenever he expressed any disappointment or frustration. She never took complaints seriously and could not validate Sam's experiences. Sam also realized that his father, as a matter of course, would always put him down in public with criticism and humiliation. Sam's father could not provide validating experiences either. Sam never thought there was any-

thing unusual about being discounted and humiliated, and assumed that was a normal part of all relationships, so he never
understood why Colleen was so "unreasonable" about his treating her that way.

Sam's experience of early relationships had become organized
into an automatic way of relating. Even though he now understood his wife's reactions, his behavior continued, but Colleen,
although she did not like his behavior and told him so, stopped
feeling guilty and responsible for it. She had always reacted to
Sam's criticisms by feeling it was her fault. In her early experiences, she was blamed for parental tensions, but now, feeling
understood and supported by me, she felt stronger and had less
need for Sam's approval. The marital balance shifted.

Colleen no longer felt it was her responsibility to take care
of Sam at her expense. She began to feel she had a right to take
care of herself, too. She could let Sam be anxious without feeling she had to turn herself inside out to reassure him. Sam,
feeling abandoned and unloved, became more anxious and, as
a result, treated Colleen more cruelly. I interpreted the intensified fighting as a manifestation of a breakdown. Sam, feeling
abandoned, became panicky. He lashed out, I interpreted, as a
desperate attempt to re-engage Colleen in the old, familiar way.
He responded to this interpretation with memories of his mother
becoming overwhelmed and yelling at him irrationally when he
did not do what she expected. His father never supported him
during his mother's tirades, and admonished him not to upset
his mother.

Sam's mother also criticized Colleen, and Colleen was furious that Sam always took his mother's side. Sam was now able
to support Colleen in their relationship with his mother, and
Colleen, for the first time, felt hopeful about the marriage. As
Sam continued to idealize me he began to see more of his father's
limitations. Feeling stronger and more sure of himself, he became assertive with his father, too.

However, Sam continued to criticize and humiliate his wife in public, and Colleen continued to use the sessions to confront him. Finally, Sam became able to see Colleen's pain, and apologized for his behavior, but he could not change it, and he felt helpless. We explored Sam's feelings of vulnerability and insecurity.

The tone of the sessions changed, and I felt that Sam and I were now doing individual psychotherapy in Colleen's presence. Colleen sat quietly and watched intently as Sam and I discussed his feelings of vulnerability in growing up. She developed a new appreciation for the depth of Sam's insecurities, and became more understanding and less critical. As she became more supportive, Sam had a realization: "Colleen and I are different." In his anxiety, he needed to see her as a twin, and he reacted to differences between them as though they were abandonments. Feeling stronger, he could now experience and talk about disappointments and frustrations without automatically translating them into betrayal and rejection.

As their relationship stabilized and Sam felt safer, he began to complain about me. He said that I joined with his wife to gang up on him and pressure him to change. He felt that I expected more progress from him, that I was disappointed in him, and that I looked down on him. He was sure that when he left my office I thought he was a "jerk." When he complained, he watched me carefully for any sign of defensiveness or irritation. He was afraid I would be hurt like his parents. When I, instead, told him that I appreciated his feedback, he felt stronger and more confident. He now got along better at home and at work, and he also could stand up for himself with his parents.

They had been coming for two years and were doing well, but were worried about finances. I thought they might be ready to be on their own, and I wondered about termination. They reacted with intense, bitter fighting, emotional distance, and great despair. Hopelessness returned and, on leaving my office, Sam turned to me and asked if I had ever been sued for starting a divorce. They were feeling abandoned by me: I had prematurely threatened to send them out on their own before they were ready to give me up.

They still idealized me and saw in me the strength they felt lacking in themselves. I was providing containing, integrating, and strengthening selfobject functions for the relationship.

I backed off, the relationship got back on track, and we continued our sessions. Sam then revealed that he felt trapped in his life style, that he wanted to change, not to work so hard, and to spend more time with his family. He wished that he could trust himself more and stop worrying so much about the future and just trust that things would work out. Gradually, he grew stronger and more confident, and able to de-idealize me. We entered the termination phase of therapy.

This last phase, lasting nine months, was ushered in by Sam's dream that we were having a session and I fell asleep. I awoke and was shocked to see that we were twenty-five minutes over our time. Listening to the dream, I wondered to myself if Sam felt he had been coming long enough and had overstayed his welcome. In his associations, Sam said he sometimes sees me nodding off in the sessions, and he feels pleased that I am human. He had given up wanting to be like his father, but he had wanted to be like me. Now he did not want to be like me either; he wanted to be himself. He no longer withdrew from Colleen when there was tension, but stayed present with her, understood her feelings, and made sure she knew he cared. He still caught himself putting her down, but now he felt bad when he saw she was hurt. "I feel I love her more," he said. Suddenly, they developed other commitments and had trouble keeping our appointments. They tapered off the sessions, and, realizing that they had the strength and courage to work on their tensions, terminated the therapy.

This therapy illustrates how couples therapy is both similar to and different from individual therapy. And it shows the contributions of self psychology in

- The application of the introspective-empathic mode of observation, the benefit of rapidly shifting and staying with each of the partner's experiences.

- Helping each partner decenter and learn to see things from the vantage point of another.
- Understanding the role of selfobject functioning between the partners of a couple, between each partner and the therapist, and between the couple as a unit and the therapist.

My doubts about the viability of their relationship were laid to rest as I came to appreciate their inner feelings of loyalty and commitment to each other.

14

Working
with Dreams

Dream is not a revelation. If a dream affords the dreamer some light on himself, it is not the person with closed eyes who makes the discovery but the person with open eyes lucid enough to fit thoughts together. Dream—a scintillating mirage surrounded by shadows—is essentially poetry.

Michel Leiris

Max Warren, a supervisor in Detroit, said to me one day, "I notice that you never do anything with dreams." I answered, "I don't know what to do with them. Sometimes I ask patients what they think about their dreams." Warren said, "That's the least helpful approach." He explained that I expected my patients to do my work, and I needed to learn the art of dream interpretation.

CLASSICAL MODEL

My theoretical perspective affected my approach. Warren had me read Freud's (1900) *Interpretation of Dreams* and he explained, "There are two dreams: the manifest dream, the dream the patient remembers, and the latent dream thoughts, the hidden ideas behind the dream." Thus I learned the classical model of dream interpretation where the manifest dream is a disguise and is of no use except as a pointer to the hidden, underlying dream-thoughts. The analyst's job is to take the manifest dream apart and to ask the patient to free associate to the different elements. Each element might lead to a different underlying meaning, and the underlying meanings represent forbidden instinctual wishes, which are cleverly disguised by the *dream work*. The dream work disguises the pent-up wishes into something ordinary and safe—like a plainclothes police officer. Once disguised, these wishes can be expressed without causing alarm and disturbing sleep.

Freud (1900) describes four processes used by the dream work to change the latent, unconscious dream-thoughts into the conscious, manifest dream. These processes are condensation, displacement, symbolization and secondary revision.

Condensation

Much compression takes place in the unconscious, and many different underlying meanings can be represented by a single element. Freud (1900) describes his dream of the "Botanical Monograph." In this dream Freud is looking at a monograph that he wrote about a plant. In the monograph he found a dried specimen of the plant preserved between the pages. The analysis of the dream showed that this one element touched on at least eight different underlying dream thoughts: (1) Freud's relationship with his wife. (He wished he gave her flowers more often.) (2) A former patient of Freud's, Frau L., whose husband forgot her birthday and her birthday flowers. (3) Freud's research on the coca plant and the use of cocaine in eye surgery. (4) A professional relationship Freud had with Professor Gärtner, whose name means gardener. (5) A memory of an incident in secondary school when Freud had trouble with a botany exam. (6) Freud's fondness for artichokes, which his wife bought for him. (7) A memory of an incident at age 5 when Freud tore the pictures out of a book his father had given him. (8) A memory of an incident at age 17 when Freud bought more books than he could pay for and suffered a humiliation at the hands of his father. One of Freud's wishes was to be famous and justify himself to his father.

This ability of the unconscious to represent many ideas with a single visual image allows for great economy in the dream work.

Displacement

A significant component of a dream-thought can be split off and displaced onto another, less significant component of the dream-thought.

Freud describes a dream where his friend R. was his uncle with a yellow beard, and Freud had a great feeling of affection for him. In his analysis of the dream Freud said that the affection he felt in the dream for R. (and his uncle) was displaced from another relationship and served here as a disguise for what in the latent dream-thoughts were critical feelings towards R., feelings that Freud was reluctant to face.

Representing significant ideas with seemingly insignificant ones is a major mechanism in disguising unconscious dream-thoughts.

Symbolization

Freud says that some images in dreams may universally represent common human experiences, and manifest content can then be directly translated into latent dream-thoughts.

For example, the king and queen in dreams will generally represent the dreamer's parents. Elongated objects may represent the penis; walking up or down steps, ladders, or staircases represents sexual intercourse; and landscapes in dreams represent genitals. Freud cautions us, however, not to use symbols arbitrarily to assume a dream's meaning. He says that we should combine our technique, "which on the one hand rests on the dreamer's associations and on the other hand fills the gaps from the interpreter's knowledge of symbols" (p. 353).

Secondary revision

Somewhere in the space between sleeping and waking, the various underlying themes, the latent dream-thoughts, are woven into a coherent story, the manifest dream. The psychic agency that fills in the gaps in the dream-thoughts and constructs this story may also contribute to the story. For example, the thought: "This is only a dream" appears, Freud says, "when the censorship, which is never quite asleep, feels that it has been taken unawares by a dream which has already been allowed through" (p. 489). The secondary revision replaces the "appearance of absurdity and disconnectedness" with an "intelligible experience" (p. 490).

Working with dreams in the classical model is similar to working with defenses and resistance. The patient is motivated to hide forbidden impulses that continually press for discharge. The analyst is the authority whose job is to ferret out, and interpret to the patient, these disguised wishes.

EGO PSYCHOLOGY

With developments in ego psychology, ego mechanisms and structures became important alongside of instinctual wishes and id mechanisms. The manifest dream now became significant. Erik Erikson (1954), in his pivotal paper "The Dream Specimen of Psychoanalysis," demonstrated the importance of the manifest dream: "Unofficially, we often interpret dreams entirely or in parts on the basis of their manifest appearance. Officially, we hurry at every confrontation with a dream to crack its manifest appearance as if it were a useless shell and to hasten to discard this shell in favor of what seems to be the more worthwhile core" (p. 17).

Erikson found that the organization of the dream's manifest content reflects the patient's personality organization, that the manifest dream has a "style of representation [that is] a reflection of the individual ego's peculiar time space, the frame of reference for all its defenses, compromises, and achievements" (p. 21). Erikson also said that "a manifest dream structure . . . on every level reflects significant trends of the dreamer's total situation" (p. 55).

Much can be learned by both patient and analyst from careful attention to the structure of the manifest dream. If a patient has an obsessional-sounding manifest dream, the patient is likely to have an obsessional personality also. Taking the manifest dream more seriously, I have found that when patients feel fragmented and disorganized, their manifest dreams will appear chaotic. When these patients feel more integrated, their manifest dreams become more organized.

SELF PSYCHOLOGY

Kohut's (1977) concept of the *self state* dream, a dream that uses "verbalizable dream-imagery to [deal with] traumatic states," further expanded on the value of the manifest dream. The dreamer attempts, Kohut says, "to deal with . . . psychological danger by covering frightening nameless processes with namable visual imagery" (p. 109).

Kohut and Wolf (1978) give an example of a patient who, feeling overburdened, might then have a dream "that he lives in a poisoned atmosphere or that he is surrounded by swarms of dangerous hornets" (p. 420). The manifest dream is not just a disguise preventing disruptions to sleep, but also serves an integrating function. It helps to process anxieties by making them accessible to cognitive strategies. In other words, if you can describe an anxiety, or give voice to a fear, you have begun the process of mastery.

Fosshage (1983) adds to our understanding of the manifest dream with his work on dreaming mentation. In the classical model, dreaming is an expression of primary process mentation, a form of ideation seen in children and in primitive cultures. This is contrasted with secondary process mentation, a more mature, symbolic form of thinking.

Instead of seeing the two types of mentation as a primitive one and a mature one, Fosshage proposes a revision where the two types, dreaming and waking mentation, exist side by side. Either type can be primitive or mature: "Implicit is a fundamental principle based on evolutionary and developmental theory that all psychic activity, i.e., waking and dreaming mentation, evolves or moves fundamentally toward higher, more complex levels of organization" (p. 657).

Fosshage (1983) defines the two types of mentation:

[Dreaming mentation or primary process] uses visual and other sensory images with intense affective colorations in serving an over-all integrative and synthetic function. Secondary process, on the other hand, is a conceptual and logical mode that makes use of linguistic symbols in serving an integrative and synthetic function. These processes may be described as different but complementary modes of apprehending, responding to, and organizing the external and internal worlds. The right-left-brain-hemisphere research that has established the functional asymmetry of the cerebral hemispheres may support this structural division. [p. 649]

In other words, we have two ways of processing ideas: visually, through the use of imagery, and symbolically, through the use of language. These two ways of processing ideas vary from person to person. For example, I find it hard to express myself with imagery, so it may be that I am too left-brained. I bought a book of similes to help me, but I still find it difficult—like shaving with an axe. (That is a simile from the book.) I envy my friends who can talk naturally with rich imagery.

Stolorow and Atwood (1982), applying the principles of psychoanalytic phenomenology, expand on our understanding of the unconscious and propose changes in our technique of dream interpretation. In classical theory, unconsciousness is maintained by repression, a defensive activity. Stolorow and Atwood propose another form of unconsciousness, the prereflective unconscious: "This form of unconsciousness is not the product of defensive activity. It results from the person's inability to recognize how the personal reality in which he lives and moves is constituted by the structures of his own subjectivity" (p. 207). This proposal suggests that early experiences take on meaning or become structuralized into organizing principles that belong to the prereflective unconscious and one way in which they can be pictured is by the manifest dream imagery.

Using these ideas, Stolorow (1978) proposes an addition to the technique of dream interpretation. The patient associates to discrete dream elements, and then Stolorow abstracts distinctive themes from the manifest dream and invites the patient to associate to those themes.

Referring to the function of dreaming, Stolorow and Atwood (1982) maintain that a central motivational principle in human psychology is the need to maintain the organization of experience. In dreaming, the concretely symbolized perceptual images of one's experiences provide a reassuring structure. Stolorow and Atwood differ from Kohut when they say that the function of self-state dreams is "not to render nameless psychological processes namable" [but to] "bring the state of the self into focal awareness with a feeling of conviction and reality that can only accompany sensory perceptions" (p. 213). In other words, if you feel fragmented and can represent that experience visually in a dream, you will feel reintegrated.

Developments in dream interpretation have expanded, but have not replaced the more traditional models. However, I now have choices: I can focus on the manifest dream, or I can approach the dream in a traditional way and ask for associations to different elements. How I choose will depend on my intuition, and if I intuitively feel there is a message in the manifest dream, I will trust my intuition and investigate further. If, however, the dream feels obscure and uncommunicative, I will assume defenses are operating and use a more traditional approach.

TECHNIQUE

When working with a dream, I start with precipitating events, affects, and my emotional reactions to the dream. Freud (1900) says that "in every dream it is possible to find a point of contact with the experiences of the previous day," and in many instances the easiest method of beginning a dream interpretation "is by looking for the event of the previous day which set it in motion" (p. 165). Something in the day's events resonates with, and is a reflection of, unconscious organizing activity. A person's way of organizing experiences will connect the present, the transference, and the past.

I do not assume literally that a dream can only be precipitated by an event from the previous day, but I often find it useful to start with the present. When I hear a dream, I might ask the patient, "When was the dream?" and then, "What happened during the day of the dream that might have precipitated it?" Often some seemingly innocuous event will have triggered the dream. Further reflection on the event reveals emotional feelings that had been discounted and not sufficiently appreciated. Sometimes the seemingly innocuous event will have been the previous therapy session.

Once I have looked for precipitants of the dream, I look to see if there are any affects in the dream. Affects are a reliable indicator of a patient's central experience. Affects, Freud (1900) said, appear in dreams relatively undisguised: ". . . the ideational material has undergone displacements and substitutions, whereas the affects have remained unaltered" (p. 460), and further stated that "affects are the constituent which is least influenced and which alone can give us a pointer as to how we should fill in the missing thoughts" (p. 461).

A patient reported a dream in which he felt hurt at not being taken seriously. When his associations to the dream did not go anywhere, I sensed resistance to transference, and asked if he felt I had not taken him seriously. At first he said that he felt I took him very seriously, but he suddenly remembered a comment I had made in our last session that made him feel discounted, and he became aware of anxiety about confronting me. He feared that I would be hurt by his complaint and would withdraw from him. To protect himself, his hurt went underground only to resurface in his dream. In this example, the previous session was the precipitant of the dream, and the underlying affects were expressed directly in the manifest dream.

Last, I try to sense my own reactions to the dream. When I resonate with some part of a dream in relation to a patient, that is where I begin investigating. Although I ask questions about precipitating events and about feelings, and ask for associations to discrete elements, I try not to ask general questions such as, "What do you think about the dream?" Patients often experience such questions as an expectation that they should know what the dream means.

A change in the analytic relationship may be reflected in a dream. For example, one reason a patient chose me for his analyst was that he thought I would be warmer and more approachable than some other analysts. He was bitterly disappointed to find me cool and distant, just like a "classical analyst." I focused on his disappointment and anger with fruitful results, but he continued to complain that he could not feel connected with me. Although focusing on the impact of my "coolness" brought forth much productive material, he continued to feel distress.

I discussed the case with James Fosshage who said, "He is having trouble feeling connected with you. When you talk to him, try leaning forward in your chair." I puzzled about that suggestion, and wondered if it would be a manipulation, but decided that a manipulation would feel unnatural, and leaning toward him when I talked felt natural and comfortable. I tried it and did not notice any difference, and the patient made no comment.

Two days later, he reported a dream: "I was in a boarding house with lots of people. We were eating dinner sitting at a long table. People were sitting on both sides of me, and I felt warm and connected." While the elements of this manifest dream point to a number of possible unconscious elements having to do with "boarding house" and "eating," I never heard any further complaints about my being cool or distant, and several months later he said he appreciated the feeling of warmth and connectedness he experienced with me. Some patients who are lying on the couch are deprived of visual contact and need help in feeling a connection. Whatever it was in my moving physically closer to him, the manifest dream clearly shows a change in his experience that reflects a change in our relationship not yet verbalized.

TRANSFERENCE

In the classical model the analyst is always assumed to be in the dream, at least latently. In the revised model of dream interpretation (Fosshage and Loew 1987), "the analyst is viewed as present only when he or she actually appears in the dream" (p. 305). But the dream will represent the way the transference relationship is organized (Stolorow and Lachmann 1984–1985). The patient's way of organizing the experience of the relationship, including the perception of the countertransference, will be reflected in the manifest dream. Rosenbaum (1965) found that the analyst appearing in the dream undisguised may represent the patient's perception of some countertransference feelings.

An example of the latter is the patient I described in Chapter 12 who came to see me because of depression following a painful divorce. She felt helpless and overwhelmed, and I found myself trying to be helpful. She then reported the dream: "I came to your office, and the door was open. I looked in and saw you sitting in your chair holding a baby in your lap."

Listening to the dream, I thought about Rosenbaum's paper and I wondered to myself if she thought I was treating her like a baby. I asked her, and she said yes, that although she felt bad, she was not as helpless as I feared. My countertransference was to be overprotective, and it made her anxious. She needed me to appreciate her pain, but not to fix it. She needed me to trust her strength and competence. The manifest dream took feelings that she was not yet consciously aware of and organized them into an image. Through the imagery I received a communication from her.

IMAGISTIC MENTATION

Because of their vivid imagery, dreams have a special appeal. I find that people who have trouble knowing what they feel cannot connect with their feelings through speech and may connect more easily through imagery. In the case of Angel, the young woman who had tried to kill herself, we became disconnected and I felt frustrated and scared. I consulted David Meltzer, a Los Angeles psychoanalyst experienced in guided imagery, and he recommended using imagery to express my feeling of disconnection with her, and suggested I say the following:

> A connection is like a stream of water that flows between us. After a while, when the stream is flowing, there is a good connection between us. Then, something happens each time when you leave. The stream dries up and all that is left is dry sand. We become disconnected. I suspect that in recent months you have been feeling increasingly disconnected from family and friends, and at the time that you tried to commit suicide it must have seemed like only dry sand everywhere; perhaps even like a sandstorm. [personal communation]

When I said that to her, she came to life, sat up in her chair, looked directly at me, and said, "A sandstorm, yes, I hadn't thought of it that way." Our connection was re-established. Talking about disconnection did not make an impression on her, but the imagery of water flowing and dry sand did. Imagistic mentation, both in imagery and in dreaming, carries a sense of conviction to patients. Imagistic mentation is the language of poets, artists, and dreamers, and it is the language analysts need to speak fluently.

15

Supervision

15

Supervision

Spoon feeding in the long run teaches us nothing but the shape of the spoon.

E. M. Forster

TEACHING TO LEARN

Teaching psychoanalysis is a major step in one's development. When I became a psychiatric resident, I supervised interns; when I became a psychoanalytic candidate, I supervised psychiatric residents; and when I became a graduate psychoanalyst, I supervised candidates. Teaching psychoanalysis has been one of my greatest learning experiences. Writing this book has been another.

My theoretical orientation at each stage of development informed my style and philosophy of supervision. When I was in a scientific mode, I supervised by teaching rules and discouraging intuition. I believed it was important for students to learn the "right" way. Gradually, I realized that many patients did well with the most awkward technique, and some patients did poorly with what appeared to be very accurate technique. Something more was going on than I could see.

Over the years I attended two supervisory workshops where the supervising analysts presented their experiences of supervision and analysis. One workshop was at a traditional psychoanalytic institute and the other was at the Institute of Contemporary Psychoanalysis in Los Angeles (ICP), an institute open to different points of view. At the first institute, each training analyst had a different idea about the presenting analyst's technique, and each presented his or her idea in a friendly but critical manner. If the analyst, for instance, used the "wrong" technique and the patient got better, it was considered to be a "transference cure" and not psychoanalysis. The focus of discussion was on which supervisor had the "truer" reality. Within a year, the attendance dwindled and the workshop was discontinued.

At the ICP workshop each training analyst also had a different idea about the presenting analyst's technique, but the tone was different. These analysts generally assessed the presentations on the gain made by the patient, even if they did not agree with the method used. At the first institute, the attitude was traditional and authoritarian—there was a right way and a wrong way. At the ICP, the stance was that if the patient and analyst were doing well together, the analyst was doing something right. The challenge was to understand how what the analyst did was helpful and to learn from the experience. Now, after five years of attendance, this is one workshop I never miss.

LEARNING TO TEACH

A challenge for supervisors is making suggestions to students that bolster confidence and encourage intuition. At the 1979 Conference on the Psychology of the Self in Los Angeles, Kohut described his supervision of a student who was a "natural" therapist. Kohut said he limited his supervisory comments to explanations of why the therapist's interventions worked. After one year of supervision, the student told Kohut that he had learned more from him than from any other supervisor. Kohut provided a validating selfobject function that aided the student's growth.

Taking my cue from Kohut, I have found that much teaching is accomplished when I can point out what my students are doing right and resist my inclination to immediately point out what they are doing wrong. I also learn much from my students when I can understand how their seemingly idiosyncratic technique is effective.

When a case is not going well, I try to assess the student's anxiety or blind spots. I review diagnostic assessment, treatment alliance, and goals. The patient may have special needs, and the student may have special needs. The student may need help in understanding and connecting with the patient. If the student's anxiety continues, I ask if the student feels pressure from me. Often the student's expectation of criticism from me is paralyzing.

One case was going well when suddenly the analyst and patient came to an impasse. I saw that the analyst had started pressuring his patient, who then shut down in response. It was clear to me what the analyst could do to get back on track, but none of my suggestions helped. I found myself annoyed and irritated with the analyst, and the supervisory relationship also came to an impasse.

When I asked the analyst if he felt pressure from me, he told me he did, with visible relief. He felt I did not trust him or appreciate his competence, and that I was trying to make him into a clone of me. I appreciated his comments, backed off, and the analytic momentum resumed. Once the analyst felt trusted by me, he started trusting his patient, and the treatment process was restored.

In another example the analyst was clearly following my suggestions and saying all the right things, but the patient was deteriorating. I began to feel helpless and frustrated, started doubting myself, and I felt worthless as a supervisor.

I asked the analyst if he felt any tension or frustration with me, and he immediately said that he resented the fee I charged him. His patient paid a low fee, and he felt it was unfair for me to charge him my full fee. I had not appreciated his dissatisfac-

tion and he did not appreciate his patient's feelings of dissatis-
faction. Once he felt I understood his feelings, he quickly became
understanding of his patient, who then made dramatic progress.
When the alliance between supervisor and analyst was restored,
the treatment alliance was then restored as well.

When a case is going well, I try to look initially at what the
student is doing that is helpful, and to make validating or acknowledging comments. This is not natural for me because of
the way I was taught. As soon as the student reports a comment
that is different from what I would have made, my impulse is
to say, without waiting to be asked, what I would have done;
but I listen to the student's interpretation and the patient's
response to it, and, resisting my natural tendency, I try to understand and to explain why it was a helpful intervention. Students
are always surprised by these explanations because they think
what is helpful is always something different from what they
are doing.

It takes time for students to learn to trust themselves, and I
want to encourage their patience. My explanations help students
because they provide a structuring experience. For example, a
supervisee told me that her patient reported repetitively, and
in great detail, an interaction with his girlfriend. When the
therapist said, "It sounds like you were feeling frustrated with
your girlfriend," the patient immediately stopped reporting and
started talking in an insightful way about his feelings. I told
the therapist that her comment was helpful. Her patient, I
explained, came in feeling disorganized and disconnected, and
his detailed, repetitive reporting was his way of using her to reorganize himself. Her comment made him feel understood, and
he felt reconnected with her and reorganized. "Oh," she said, "I
didn't realize he felt disorganized and disconnected." She was
pleased, and she felt effective.

I used to worry that not commenting on what looked like
errors in technique was negligence. I have since learned that if
I am patient, students will come to feel safe and will bring in
more detailed examples of their interactions with their patients

and look to me for comments. These provide ample opportunity to make suggestions. For example, if a student asks what I think about an interpretation, I might say that it was accurate, but it focused only on content, and that one could also focus on the affect.

One patient, near the end of her first year of analysis, asked, "How much longer do you think this analysis will take?" The analyst groaned inwardly, thinking, "We've been through this before; I already told her it could easily take four years." But he answered her: "What brings this up now?" "My husband wants to know," she said. She explained that her husband can do better financially if they move, and he wants to know how much longer they will be tied down because of her analysis.

The patient has a problem with intimacy, and one defense is to talk about moving away. The analyst felt that she was hiding behind her husband by talking about his feelings about moving instead of her own. "My husband said he didn't think I was that sick," she added, implying that needing analysis was a sign of illness, something shameful. The analyst asked her if her focusing on her husband's feelings covered her own fears of making a commitment, including a commitment to the analysis.

The analyst asked me what I thought about his interpretation. I said he was accurate, her response was positive, and that they did a good piece of analytic work. I then said that he had focused only on the content, on her way of protecting herself, and that I might have also focused on her affect, that she felt ashamed and defective.

I explained that investigating and understanding her feeling of shame could lead to a deeper understanding of her fear of committing herself in a relationship. She worries, for example, what others think about her, and she anticipates rejection if she doesn't perform. It may be, I speculated, that if she got closer to her husband, or to her analyst, she would feel more vulnerable to being exposed. If her self-experience is one of defect or inadequacy, then keeping her distance protects her from the shame and humiliation of being exposed.

The analyst recalled that when his patient was little, she had to perform and to be "good" to maintain her parents' interest. Her parents, unfortunately, did not remain interested in her, and she believed it was because of her deficiencies. The analyst's thinking now crystallized. "That's very helpful. I understand what I am trying to do, and I have a better idea now of how to do it," he said, and was pleased that he was doing well. He felt he had learned something new that would enrich his work.

UNCONSCIOUS COMMUNICATION

A different challenge for me was the analyst who was overprotective and was giving her patient advice and reassurance. I wanted to tell her to stop, that she was being supportive and unanalytic, but I waited, contained myself, and listened. I could hear that her patient was making progress. I pointed that out, and she was pleased.

Then I asked her if she worried about her patient. "I like him," she said. "I don't want him to be hurt." I had a picture of vulnerability. I was feeling vulnerable as a supervisor: my student would do a bad job and it would reflect on me. The student felt vulnerable: her patient would get hurt, and it would be her failure. Perhaps we were both reacting to some feeling of vulnerability in the patient.

"Do you think he feels vulnerable?" I asked her. "Yes," she said, "he fears being a failure." Despite the patient's many successes and accomplishments, he continued to feel inadequate and incompetent. The analyst now saw his feeling of vulnerability as something to explore, so she stopped reassuring and started investigating. A theme then emerged in which the patient experienced his mother as helpless and vulnerable, and he had felt pressure to take care of and reassure her.

My initial reaction was not to trust my student and to tell her what to do the way she was telling her patient what to do. Once I contained my anxiety and trusted her, she became able to trust her patient. As a result, he felt stronger and the ana-

lytic process deepened. The analyst and I both came to understand that the patient was identifying with his helpless mother,
and she and I were both identifying with his feeling of pressure
to fix his mother and not to feel like a failure. Similar invariant
organizing principles were activated in each of us. The analyst
and I both used our countertransference feelings to deepen our
understanding of the analytic material. When I could refrain
from "fixing" the analyst, she became able to refrain from "fixing" her patient. The patient, in turn, eventually became able
to refrain from "fixing" his mother and his wife.

The intimacy of the analytic relationship lends itself to subtle
communications between patient and analyst, many of which
are not conscious. Listening to clinical material, either directly
from the patient or indirectly through the supervisee, evokes
images and feelings, a countertransference response, in the listener. The countertransference is determined, in part, by the
listener's unconscious organizing principles. If these resonate
with the patient's unconscious organizing principles, a powerful communication can take place, as in the case where the
analyst and I each touched on feelings of vulnerability.

When the supervisor's reactions are neutral or counter-
resonant with the treating analyst's reactions, a frustrating disjunction can occur. An analyst reported to me that his patient
asserted himself: "I want better treatment. I'm tired of being
pushed around. I'm beginning to realize how much my father
always pushed me around." The patient then hesitated, and
said, "Maybe I just set myself up for it. Maybe I like being pushed
around. Maybe that's what I need." The analyst interpreted that
getting pushed around was his way of maintaining a connection. He set himself up for abuse so he would not have to be
alone.

I said that the interpretation was accurate, but I suspected
it was distant from the patient's experience. I wondered if the
patient might not feel criticized by the interpretation, and explained that I noticed a shift in affect when the patient started
complaining about his father. The patient said he wanted better

treatment and started to talk about mistreatment by his father. Suddenly, it seemed to me, he was putting himself down. "Maybe I just set myself up," he said. Was there something about complaining about his father, I wondered, that made him anxious, and was it safer to put himself down at that point?

"I don't think he was putting himself down," the analyst said, "I think he was being insightful." Now the analyst and I were at a disjunction. I could agree that the patient's comment was insightful, but I also felt there was something inherently humiliating or demeaning in saying, "Maybe I just set myself up."

If the analyst could have understood it that way, I might have suggested saying something like, "Of course you set yourself up. That's the price you feel you have to pay to ensure a connection. If you assert yourself, you will end up alone and isolated." But the analyst did not agree that there was any put-down involved. He thought that was how people were; they had to face that and take responsibility for it. That was one of his invariant organizing principles. I suspected that was how he experienced his analyst as treating him, but my job was to give my opinion and then move on to some area where we could find a conjunction.

In this case, the analyst subsequently became sensitive to subtle shifts in affect in his patient. He learned to focus on these shifts, identify their precipitants, and uncover their unconscious meanings. Finding areas of conjunction where the analyst and I can agree is where the teaching takes place.

Taking what we learn from teachers and from experience, and sharing it with others, helps us organize and integrate our knowledge. The more we teach, the more we learn. I used to wonder why my mentor, Bernard Brandchaft, made regular trips from Los Angeles to San Diego for our seminars on self psychology. It certainly was not for the insignificant amount of money we paid him. Now I realize that he was developing his ideas and he was using us to further his own creative process.

16

Hazards
and Rewards

What are we hoping to get out of it—is it really just for the sake of a gloved hand waving at you from a golden coach?

John Osborne

Psychoanalysis helps me to learn; I wrote this book to help me learn. Both are hard work, but the rewards are great, and I would like to set forth in this final chapter a review of those challenges and benefits.

Psychoanalysis is one of the few professions where we can continually improve our skills and face new challenges. The occupational hazards of psychoanalysis include a sense of isolation, the fear of litigation, the difficulty of dealing with hopelessness, and the frustration of being in a "no-win" situation.

ISOLATION

The psychoanalytic relationship is a professional relationship, not a social one. We work one to one with patients in a restrained way, and when we leave our offices we cannot, because of ethical considerations, talk to friends and family about our work. To deal with the isolation we must rely on colleagues. Professional societies, peer supervision groups, and study groups provide safe outlets where we can talk openly about, and master, our frustrations and fears. When a patient is well known, however, we must go outside of our community.

I remember when Ralph Greenson, the Los Angeles psychoanalyst, described how he dealt with his state of mind while treating Marilyn Monroe's depression during the period before her death. "I have a friend, a psychoanalyst in another city," Greenson said, "and once a week I called him long distance." Greenson told his friend not to say anything, just to listen, and he would talk for an hour, thank his friend, and hang up. That is how Greenson dealt with the pressures of treating his famous patient.

Trying to deal with patient pressures by yourself is unrealistic, but supervisors who always know better and keep telling you what to do are also to be avoided. Colleagues and supervisors who can offer helpful suggestions and, at the same time, can support your efforts and encourage you to hang in with your patient are to be prized above all.

LITIGATION FEARS

Fears of a patient committing suicide put enormous pressure on a psychoanalyst, and fears of litigation can paralyze a psychoanalyst's therapeutic function. Analysts more and more find themselves walking a fine line between doing good practice and protecting themselves.

Unusually difficult cases can often pressure and stretch a therapist's endurance. Therapists feeling such pressures may benefit from having the vantage point of an outside consultant. In one case that I had the privilege of supervising, the fear of a lawsuit stimulated a countertransference reaction that led to a disruption and an impasse. It was not until I stepped in as a consultant and assumed co-responsibility for the patient that the therapist felt freed up and could re-establish the therapeutic connection.

At age 20, Linda entered therapy with a newly licensed therapist who did not initially appreciate the scope of Linda's disturbance. Sexually and emotionally abused as a child, Linda was now vulnerable to disabling depressions and suicidal preoccupations, which she tried to self-medicate with drugs and alcohol. Linda also tried containing episodes of depersonalization and dissociation through acts of self-cutting, burning, and laxative abuse. Several involuntary hospitalizations during adolescence only exacerbated her problems.

In the first phase of therapy, lasting three years, Linda had difficulty talking and spent much of the time in silence. Gradually feeling safe with her therapist, she began talking about her inner life. The emergence of painful memories frightened her; verbalizing them helped her feel a sense of mastery. At times, however, Linda's inner chaos became overwhelming, and on one occasion she took a medication overdose but refused hospitalization. The therapist consulted me, we decided not to hospitalize Linda against her will, and supervision began.

In the middle phase of therapy, lasting eight years, the therapist spent much time attuning to and helping Linda develop a vocabulary to describe her feelings. I helped the therapist further understand the patient's experiences and fragmented communications. "It was like deciphering hieroglyphics," the therapist said.

My task was also to support and sustain the therapist, who struggled with her own reactions to Linda's despair. She discovered that attempts to introduce hope or make suggestions prematurely were catastrophic; Linda felt discounted and became disorganized. She needed to experience and master overwhelming feelings of fear, hopelessness, and despair that she had suffered when abused as a child—feelings that had been sequestered to protect herself from conflict with her mother. She needed the therapist to understand her hopelessness and not pressure her—as her mother had done—to comply with the therapist's expectations to feel better.

Linda suffered from chronic psychic pain—from anguish and inner chaos—yet a variety of treatment approaches, including medication, had failed to bring relief. Linda did not want to die, but she needed to know that, should the pain become unbearable, killing herself was a way to bring relief. The therapist's task was to appreciate and contain Linda's hopelessness and despair *and* understand that the only way Linda could continue to live and stay connected in the therapy was to keep suicide as an escape.

Eight years into the analytic work a crisis occurred. Although Linda suffered setbacks after each step forward, she was improving and was able to talk about her experiences and feelings. Then, after a Christmas visit to her parents, she mysteriously deteriorated. Her suicidal gestures intensified, she refused to leave the office at the end of sessions, and she made constant telephone calls to the therapist.

As her patient deteriorated, the therapist began to feel overly responsible and found it difficult to set limits. Sessions ran overtime, telephone calls were hard to end, and the therapist found she was overextending herself in an effort to catch the patient's fall. She did not know how to balance her patient's needs with her legitimate needs. In the supervision I said that Linda had gotten over setbacks before, and we had to trust that she would get through this one, too. I did not know if Linda would get through it, but from my vantage point I did know that staying connected with Linda was the only help the therapist had to offer.

The therapist's fears mobilized an unconscious organizing principle in me where I felt pressure to fix her anxiety. To protect myself I minimized her concern and did not realize she was losing confidence in herself and in me. As a result, she sought consultation with other colleagues, one of whom criticized her for working with someone who was so disturbed. Another said she was putting herself at risk legally, and should her patient succeed in killing herself, she could be held responsible. Another suggested she should refer Linda to another therapist.

Not wanting to abandon her patient, yet feeling alone and vulnerable, the therapist asked me to see Linda. Her plan was to reduce her sessions from three times a week to twice a week and have Linda see me once a week. Then if Linda killed herself, I would be responsible too. I agreed.

In successful analytic work, previously thwarted developmental strivings will be awakened, and unconscious organizing principles will be set in motion in the patient, in the analyst, and in the supervisor. Linda's needs and demands had activated in the therapist the unconscious organizing principle from her childhood that she was supposed to take care of others before taking care of herself. Once the therapist could identify this process in herself, she was able to remain firm in her decision to have Linda see me, despite Linda's vigorous protestations that she was being abandoned.

CONSULTATIONS

I told Linda and the therapist that my job was to help them restore their relationship, and I met with Linda weekly for seven months and then monthly for ten months. Three themes emerged from this work:

The first theme was a series of complaints about the therapist. Linda did not want to see me, and she only came because she was being forced. The therapist had made seeing me a condition for continuing her therapy. "Now I have to take care of her," Linda complained. "I have enough to take care of without having to take care of her, too!" she cried. "I'm sorry she's burnt out," Linda lamented, "but what about me?"

The second theme was a series of tests. As Linda complained, I tried to understand her point of view. "Of course you feel unfairly treated," I said. "You have to drive a long distance to see me and pay me money you can't afford just to take care of your therapist." Linda felt understood, became teary, and then, without warning, jumped up and ran out the door. In the next session, anticipating my criticism, she apologized for leaving abruptly and put herself down. I told her that leaving made sense, that feeling understood made her feel closer to me and more vulnerable to being hurt by me, and that running out was how she protected herself.

The next session, Linda arrived with her dog, a small French poodle who, she announced, hated men. To her surprise, and mine, the dog jumped up into my lap and spent most of the session snuggled against my arm. Linda then revealed the depth of her attachment to her dog and the importance of their relationship. She worried about the dog's anorexia and told me how she dealt with getting the dog to eat. In subsequent sessions she sometimes brought the dog and sometimes did not, but I always looked forward to her visits. And the following Christmas, after we stopped meeting, I received a lovely Christmas card from the two of them.

The third theme was the gradual sharing of memories of early abuse and molest. Complaining to me about her therapist and being taken seriously was a new experience for Linda, and she discussed the impossibility of complaining to her mother. Linda was raped by her uncle when she was a little girl, and when she reported the rape to her mother, she was scolded. "You are evil," her mother said. "God put you on earth to serve as a lesson for others." She tried turning to her father for support, and that angered her mother. "You're going to give him a heart attack," her mother said. When I observed that her mother had difficulty seeing her as a separate person, she said: "In my family you are just their property for them to use."

The complaints about her therapist diminished, and feeling now that she deserved better treatment from her family, Linda talked about injuries by her mother. Talking about the pain often helped her feel better integrated, but sometimes she became overwhelmed with guilt and, after certain sessions, she cut herself. She told me she felt hopeless, but she never looked to me for reassurance and I never gave any. I felt most connected with her, though, when she told me about her hopelessness.

After one year, Linda was able to tell the therapist about the traumatic visit home where she told her mother about the rape and triggered the crisis. Her deterioration now became understandable. Linda believed that if she told her therapist what happened when she returned from her visit with her parents, the therapist, like her mother, would also turn on her and not believe that she had been raped. As a result of this impossible bind, she felt disconnected and disorganized, and she escalated the self-destructive behavior in a desperate attempt at self-containment.

In our last session she told me her insurance benefits had run out and she offered me her dog in lieu of payment. She did not want to see me, but felt she had to because of her agreement with her therapist. I wondered if this humiliated her, and she said that it did. "I should never have agreed to this," she said, and she stormed out.

The therapist had expected me to defer payment as she had done, and was disappointed that I had not done so. Now she had to decide whether to refer Linda elsewhere, or whether she should see Linda without my direct involvement. Feeling that she was now able to make such a decision, she no longer felt trapped and agreed to continue the therapy. She reserved the option, however, of changing her mind should she again feel trapped and overwhelmed. This paralleled Linda's experience and her need to continue therapy as long as she had her escape hatch—suicide.

Linda continued to develop in emotional strength, independence, and self-confidence. I subsequently found out that she felt protected by seeing both the therapist and me, as if she had two parents, one who "held" her while she worked out her tensions with the other one—a new, developmental experience. My assuming co-responsibility for Linda helped the therapist expand her endurance, contain her fear of litigation, and resolve a serious treatment impasse.

The threat of litigation hangs over our heads like a toxic cloud. While it is hard to predict who might sue us, the best protection against litigation is to keep careful records and to consult regularly with colleagues and supervisors.

HOPELESSNESS

The hardest challenge for any analyst is treating hopelessness. To stay connected with a patient's hopelessness means to feel our own hopelessness. Therapists fear that understanding hopelessness will encourage suicide, but patients do not commit suicide because they feel hopeless; they commit suicide because they feel hopeless and alone. As long as patients feel understood in their hopelessness and connected with another person, they will stay alive.

I learned this from a depressed, young attorney, who after two months of analysis, said that his professional life was much improved, but in his personal life, he still felt lonely and isolated. His depression deepened, and each of my interpretations left him feeling more hopeless, though I believed I understood him. I, too, came to feel hopeless. I tried harder. I pointed out the improvements in his professional life, but he got worse. He decided to quit therapy and in the last session, as he was about to leave, he turned to me and asked in a plaintive voice, "What would you do if you were in my shoes?"

I was taken aback, thought for a moment, and became aware of my own hopelessness and despair. I said, "I realize I haven't appreciated the depth of your isolation and hopelessness or your inability to get relief from the pain, and if I were in your shoes I would be desperate for relief. I would want to kill myself." He relaxed; warmth returned to his voice, and he said, "Now you understand." Our treatment alliance was restored, and the analysis progressed to a successful conclusion.

THE "NO-WIN" EXPERIENCE

Treatment is a delicate balance. When patients experience us as understanding, they reveal more painful experiences, and anticipate the perfect understanding they failed to receive in infancy. No therapist can understand perfectly, and disappointments are inevitable. Patients often experience these disappointments as disruptions and may feel hurt or frightened, or sometimes injured and betrayed, and present therapists with a dilemma. If they feel guilty and try harder to be more understanding, the patient may experience a seduction, a promise that the longings for perfect understanding will be fulfilled. Yet if the therapist does not try harder, the patient may feel abandoned and rejected, and believe that the therapist no longer cares.

Sometimes no matter which tack we take, our patients will despair and feel hopeless, and will anticipate that their complaints will drive us away or move us to criticize them. If we feel guilty and try harder, they feel anxious and worry they have hurt us. If we stay calm, they feel abandoned and complain that we do not care. Inadvertently, we end up reliving with them an early traumatic situation of injury or rejection.

OPPORTUNITY

These painful experiences of disruption in treatment are not brought about intentionally, but when they occur, they provide opportunities for new developmental experiences. One opportunity is to have an experience of being taken seriously. Our attempts to understand, from the patient's point of view, how we have hurt them, and our taking their complaints seriously without being defensive or blaming, helps to heal the disruption and to provide a new developmental experience.

I saw this in my work with Linda's therapist when the supervisory relationship became disrupted. When the therapist expressed her disappointment in me for not being able to do more with Linda, I took her seriously and was neither defensive about my "failure" nor critical of her for "expecting so much." Our relationship was restored and she in turn became more confident, and more understanding of Linda's criticisms. Their relationship was also restored. And as her therapist felt stronger and more confident in the face of Linda's complaints, Linda became stronger and better able to stand up for herself in relationships with peers and employers. Her arrested development of self-confidence and self-worth was back on track.

It may be hard to imagine that unbearable hopelessness and overwhelming psychic pain can be a treatment opportunity, but if you think of a small child with a limited vocabulary who is being raped, what words can the child use to describe the experience? Caregivers must work very hard to help the child process—talk about and master—the pain, the rage, the helplessness, the fear, and the humiliation. If caregivers cannot listen or, instead, discount or criticize the child, then the child must learn to disavow or sequester the feelings.

As adults in therapy, these individuals will, when they feel safe and connected, use the therapist to help process this early pain and fear. The hopelessness and despair that now arise may represent feelings experienced during repeated molest when no adult figure was available for help and protection. How can a therapist attune to or stay connected with the experiences of a small child with little or no vocabulary?

That is the challenge. We can try talking about anger or rage, but these terms rarely fit the child's experience, and our patient feels more distant and alone. However, allowing ourselves to feel our own shame and failure, to stay with our own hopelessness and despair, can bring us closer to our patient's inner emotional world and early childhood experiences.

The abused child suffers two traumas: abuse and isolation. When attempts by the child to talk about the abuse pushes parental figures away, the child is deprived of the opportunity to process the pain and fear. The child learns to disavow the pain to preserve essential relationships.

Painful experiences of hopelessness and despair can provide a special opportunity for a deeper level of communication between analyst and patient. When I feel stuck in a no-win situation, I wonder if my experience in some way parallels or reflects the patient's early experience. Perhaps my patient felt she could not win with her mother. The mother may have gotten upset and looked to her daughter for relief. If the daughter tried to "fix" her mother, and her mother continued to be unhappy, the little girl felt like a failure. If she left her mother to take care of herself, she was subjected to accusations of not caring and of being selfish. The child could not win.

When two people, a parent and a child, or a patient and a therapist, develop a close connectedness, they can communicate internal feeling states in nonverbal ways. Exactly how this takes place, I do not know, but I do believe that carefully monitoring one's internal feeling state while with a patient can often provide clues to the patient's internal feeling state. I do not assume automatically that what I am feeling represents the patient's feeling, but I use my reactions as a pointer to where I want to address my investigation.

FRUITS

People ask why I bother treating such difficult patients, pointing out that the process is slow and stormy, and the risks are high. With a patient like Linda, the treatment could be a success and the patient could still die because there has been so much damage. I answer that my development proceeds in tandem with my patient's development, and I have never had a patient experience significant change or growth without some parallel change or growth in myself. The work never becomes dull or routine. One of my teachers, the Los Angeles psychoanalyst Rudolph Ekstein, once said that we were like the natives who live at the foot of Mt. Etna, the volcano. Every twenty years or so, it erupts and destroys the village. When someone asked why they keep rebuilding their village in the same spot and not in a safer spot a few miles away, a native answered, "Because here is where we grow the choicest grapes."

References

Atwood, E., and Stolorow, R. (1979). *Faces in a Cloud: Inter-subjectivity in Personality Theory*. Northvale, NJ: Jason Aronson.

———— (1984). *Structures of Subjectivity: Explorations in Psychoanalytic Phenomenology*. Hillsdale, NJ: Analytic Press.

Bacal, H. (1985). Optimal responsiveness and the therapeutic process. In *Progress in Self Psychology*, vol. 1, ed. A. Goldberg, pp. 202–227. New York: Guilford.

Bacal, H., and Thomson, P. G. (1993). The psychoanalyst's selfobject needs and the effect of their frustration on the treatment: A new view of countertransference. Paper presented at the 16th Annual Conference on the Psychology of the Self, Toronto, October 31.

Brandchaft, B. (1983). The negativism of the negative therapeutic reaction and the psychology of the self. In *The Future of Psychoanalysis: Essays in honor of Heinz Kohut*, ed. A. Goldberg, pp. 327–359. New York: International Universities Press.

———— (1993). To free the spirit from its cell. In *Progress in Self Psychology*, vol. 9, ed. A. Goldberg, pp. 209–230. New York: Guilford.

Brandchaft, B., and Stolorow, R. (1984a). A current perspective on difficult patients. In *Kohut's Legacy: Contributions to Self Psychology*, ed. P. E. Stepansky and A. Goldberg, pp. 93–115. Hillsdale, NJ: Analytic Press.

_____ (1984b). The borderline concept: pathological character or iatrogenic myth? In *Empathy II*, ed. J. Lichtenberg, M. Bornstein, and D. Silver, pp. 333–357. Hillsdale, NJ: Analytic Press.

Brenner, C. (1959). The masochistic character: genesis and treatment. *Journal of the American Psychoanalytic Association* 7:197–226.

Bush, M. (1989). The role of unconscious guilt in psychopathology and psychotherapy. *Bulletin of the Menninger Clinic* 53:97–107.

Carder, S. L. (1991). Clinical case description of a segment of a psychoanalytic experience. *International Journal of Psycho-Analysis* 72:383–392.

Curtis, H. C. (1990). The patient as existential victim: a classical view. *Psychoanalytic Inquiry* 10:498–508.

Curtis, J. T., Silberschatz, G., Sampson, H., et al. (1988). Developing reliable psychodynamic case formulations: an illustration of the plan diagnosis method. *Psychotherapy* 27:513–521.

Eagle, M. (1993). Enactments, transference, and symptomatic cure—a case history. *Psychoanalytic Dialogues* 3:93–110.

Erikson, E. H. (1954). The dream specimen of psychoanalysis. *Journal of the American Psychoanalytic Association* 2:5–56.

Fosshage, J. L. (1983). The psychological function of dreams: a revised psychoanalytic perspective. *Psychoanalysis and Contemporary Thought* 6:641–669.

_____ (1990). How theory shapes technique: perspectives on a self-psychological clinical presentation—clinical protocol. *Psychoanalytic Inquiry* 10:461–477.

_____ (1994). Toward reconceptualising transference: theoretical and clinical considerations. *International Journal of Psycho-Analysis* 75:265–280.

Fosshage, J. L., and Loew, C. A., eds. (1987). *Dream Interpretation: A Comparative Study, Revised Edition*. New York: PMA.

Freud, S. (1900). The interpretation of dreams. *Standard Edition* 4/5:1–626.

———— (1905). Fragment of an analysis of a case of hysteria. *Standard Edition* 7:1–63.

———— (1910). "Wild" psycho-analysis. *Standard Edition* 11:219–227.

———— (1912). Recommendations to physicians practicing psychoanalysis. *Standard Edition* 12:109–120.

———— (1913). On beginning the treatment. *Standard Edition* 12:121–144.

———— (1919). "A child is being beaten": a contribution to the study of the origin of sexual perversions. *Standard Edition* 17:175–204.

———— (1923). The ego and the id. *Standard Edition* 19:1–66.

———— (1926). Inhibitions, symptoms and anxiety. *Standard Edition* 20:75–175.

Friedman, L. (1988). *The Anatomy of Psychotherapy*. Hillsdale, NJ: Analytic Press.

Gassner, S., Sampson, H., Weiss, J., and Brumer, S. (1982). The emergence of warded-off contents. *Psychoanalysis and Contemporary Thought* 5:55–75.

Gill, M. (1954). Psychoanalysis and exploratory psychotherapy. *Journal of the American Psychoanalytic Association* 2:771–797.

———— (1984). Psychoanalysis and psychotherapy: a revision. *International Review of Psycho-Analysis* 11:161–180.

Goldberg, A., and Marcus, D. (1985). Natural termination: some comments on ending analysis without setting a date. *Psychoanalytic Quarterly* 54:46–65.

Greenson, R. R. (1967). *The Technique and Practice of Psychoanalysis*. Vol. 1. New York: International Universities Press.

Hamilton, V. (1991). Patterns of transference interpretation: an empirical study. *The British Psycho-Analytical Society Bulletin* 27:1–14.

Hoffman, I. Z. (1994). Dialectical thinking and therapeutic action in the psychoanalytic process. *Psychoanalytic Quarterly* 63:187–218.

Kohut, H. (1959). Introspection, empathy, and psychoanalysis: an examination of the relationship between mode of observation and theory. *Journal of the American Psychoanalytic Association* 7:459–483.

——— (1971). *The Analysis of the Self*. New York: International Universities Press.

——— (1977). *The Restoration of the Self*. New York: International Universities Press.

——— (1982). Introspection, empathy, and the semi-circle of mental health. *International Journal of Psycho-Analysis* 63:395–408.

——— (1984). *How Does Analysis Cure?* Chicago: University of Chicago Press.

Kohut, H., and Wolf, E. S. (1978). The disorders of the self and their treatment: an outline. *International Journal of Psycho-Analysis* 59:413–425.

Lachmann, F. M. (1986). Interpretation of psychic conflict and adversarial relationships: a self-psychological perspective. *Psychoanalytic Psychology* 3:341–355.

Lichtenberg, J. (1989). *Psychoanalysis and Motivation*. Hillsdale, NJ: Analytic Press.

——— (1994). How libido theory shaped technique. *Journal of the American Psychoanalytic Association* 42:727–739.

Lichtenberg, J. D., Lachmann, F. M., and Fosshage, J. L. (1992). *Self and Motivational Systems: Toward a Theory of Psychoanalytic Technique*. Hillsdale, NJ: Analytic Press.

Lindon, J. A. (1991). Does technique require theory? *Bulletin of the Menninger Clinic* 55:1–21.

Mahler, M. S., Pine, F., and Bergman, A. (1975). *The Psychological Birth of the Human Infant*. New York: Basic Books.

Malin, A. (1993). A self-psychological approach to the treatment of resistance: a case report. *International Journal of Psycho-Analysis* 74:505–518.

Malin, N. (1990). Returning to psychotherapy with the same therapist: a self psychological perspective. *Clinical Social Work Journal* 18:115–129.

Menninger, K., and Holzman, P. S. (1973). *Theory of Psychoanalytic Technique*. New York: Basic Books.

Moore, B. E., and Fine, B. D. (1968). *A Glossary of Psychoanalytic Terms and Concepts*. New York: American Psychoanalytic Association.

Ornstein, A. (1991). The dread to repeat: comments on the working through process in psychoanalysis. *Journal of the American Psychoanalytic Association* 39: 377–398.

Ornstein, P. H., and Ornstein, A. (1985). Clinical understanding and explaining: the empathic vantage point. In *Progress in Self Psychology*, vol. 1, ed. A. Goldberg, pp. 43–61. New York: Guilford.

Random House Unabridged Dictionary, Second Edition (1983). New York: Random House.

Rangell, L. (1954). Reporter—Panel Report: Psychoanalysis and dynamic psychotherapy—similarities and differences. *Journal of the American Psychoanalytic Association* 2:152–166.

Rosenbaum, M. (1965). Dreams in which the analyst appears undisguised—a clinical and statistical study. *International Journal of Psycho-Analysis* 46:429–437.

Sandler, J. (1983). Reflections on some relations between psychoanalytic concepts and psychoanalytic practice. *International Journal of Psycho-Analysis* 64:35–45.

Schafer, R. (1974). Talking to patients in psychotherapy. *Bulletin of the Menninger Clinic* 38:503–515.

Schwaber, E. (1981). Empathy: a mode of analytic listening. *Psychoanalytic Inquiry* 1:357–392.

_____ (1983a). Psychoanalytic listening and psychic reality. *International Review of Psycho-Analysis* 10:379–392.

_____ (1983b). Construction, reconstruction, and the mode of clinical attunement. In *The Future of Psychoanalysis*, ed. A. Goldberg, pp. 273–291. New York: International Universities Press.

Shane, M. (1979). The developmental approach to "working through" in the analytic process. *International Journal of Psycho-Analysis* 60:375–382.

Shapiro, S. (1989). The provocative masochistic patient—an intersubjective approach to treatment. *Bulletin of the Menninger Clinic* 53:319–330.

_____ (1991). Affect integration in psychoanalysis: a clinical approach to self destructive behavior. *Bulletin of the Menninger Clinic* 55:363–374.

Silverman, L. H. (1989). Commentary on a new view of unconscious guilt. *Bulletin of the Menninger Clinic* 53:135–142.

Socarides, D. D., and Stolorow, R. (1984/85). Affects and selfobjects. *The Annual of Psychoanalysis* 12/13:105–119. Madison, CT: International Universities Press.

Stolorow, R. (1975). The narcissistic function of masochism (and sadism). *International Journal of Psycho-Analysis* 56:441–448.

_____ (1978). Themes in dreams. *International Journal of Psycho-Analysis* 59:473–475.

_____ (1992). Subjectivity and self psychology: a personal odyssey. In *Progress in Self Psychology*, vol. 8, ed. A. Goldberg, pp. 241–250. New York: Guilford.

Stolorow, R., and Atwood, G. (1982). Psychoanalytic phenomenology of the dream. *The Annual of Psychoanalysis* 10:205–220.

_____ (1992). *Contexts of Being: The Intersubjective Foundations of Psychological Life*. Hillsdale, NJ: Analytic Press.

Stolorow, R., Atwood, G., and Ross, J. (1978). The representational world in psychoanalytic therapy. *International Review of Psycho-Analysis* 5:247–256.

Stolorow, R., Brandchaft, B., and Atwood, G. (1987). *Psychoana-lytic Treatment: An Intersubjective Approach*. Hillsdale, NJ: Analytic Press.

Stolorow, R., and Lachmann, F. (1980). *Psychoanalysis of Developmental Arrests: Theory and Treatment*. New York: International Universities Press.

_____ (1984–1985). Transference: the future of an illusion. *The Annual of Psychoanalysis* 12–13:19–38. New York: International Universities Press.

Trop, J. (1994). Self psychology and intersubjectivity theory. In *The Intersubjective Perspective*, ed. R. D. Stolorow, G. E. Atwood, and B. Brandchaft, pp. 77–91. Northvale, NJ: Jason Aronson.

Trop, J., and Stolorow, R. (1991). A developmental perspective on analytic empathy. *Journal of the American Academy of Psychoanalysis* 19:31–46.

Weiss, J. (1993). *How Psychotherapy Works: Process and Technique*. New York: Guilford.

Weiss, J., Sampson, H., and the Mount Zion Psychotherapy Research Group. (1986). *The Psychoanalytic Process: Theory, Clinical Observations and Empirical Research*. New York: Guilford.

Winnicott, D. W. (1960a). The theory of the parent–infant relationship. In *The Maturational Processes and the Facilitating Environment*, pp. 37–55, New York: International Universities Press, 1965.

_____ (1960b). Ego distortion in terms of true and false self. In *The Maturational Processes and the Facilitating Environment*, pp. 140–152. New York: International Universities Press, 1965.

Wolf, E. (1988). *Treating the Self*. New York: Guilford.

Zinsser, W. (1988). *Writing to Learn*. New York: Harper & Row.

Index

159